Making Liturgy

About the Editors and Contributors

Dorothea McEwan, a historian, is Archivist in The Warburg Institute, University of London. She was a founder member of the 'British School of Feminist Theology' and the journal *Feminist Theology*. She is the author of *Women Experiencing Church*, *Introducing Feminist Theology* (with Lisa Isherwood) and *An A to Z of Feminist Theology* (with Lisa Isherwood). She is a member of Catholic Women's Ordination, of Women's Ordination Worldwide and a former member of the International Committee of the European Women's Synod.

Pat Pinsent is a lecturer and researcher at the University of Surrey Roehampton, and currently specializes in children's literature, the subject of most of the seven books she has written or edited. She was a founding member of the Catholic Women's Network in 1984 and for much of the period since then she has edited *Network*, the quarterly journal of the organization.

Ianthe Pratt runs the London Christian Women's Resource Centre. She is Chair of the Association for Inclusive Language, is involved in the work of Catholic Women's Ordination and St Joan's International Alliance, and has written a number of books on liturgy with her husband, Oliver Pratt.

Veronica Seddon was a member of the team which planned the women's conference, 'Called to Full Humanity' in 1984 at which the Catholic Women's Network was set up. Since then she has been a member of the Core Planning group and is also the convenor of the Women Gather for Worship group, a CWN initiative. For ten years, it has provided an opportunity for women to experience and participate in liturgy and learn how to create their own.

Ann Farr trained in theology but has moved into teaching children with special needs. Her interest in liturgies stems from her involvement with the Justice and Peace movement.

Gillian Limb has worked in ecumenical lay ministry initiating several liturgy groups. She is co-founder of the Wherwell Liturgy group and an Associate member of the Iona Community. She works for the Anglican Councils of Social Responsibility in the Dioceses of Winchester and Portsmouth as a Core Group Adviser.

Myra Poole is a member of Catholic Women's Network, Catholic Women's Ordination and on the Steering Committee of Women's Ordination Worldwide; she represents CWO on the European Network. She is the author of *Prayer, Protest, Power: The Spirituality of Julie Billiart Today* (Canterbury Press).

June Boyce-Tillman is Professor of Applied Music at King Alfred's College, Winchester.

Lala Winkley is a trained drama teacher, and has made use of her creative skills in this area in devising liturgies over a long period of time.

Making Liturgy

Creating Rituals for Worship and Life

Edited by
Dorothea McEwan, Pat Pinsent,
Ianthe Pratt and Veronica Seddon

CANTERBURY
PRESS
Norwich

First published in 2001 by the Canterbury Press Norwich
(a publishing imprint of Hymns Ancient & Modern Limited,
a registered charity)
St Mary's Works
St Mary's Plain
Norwich, Norfolk, NR3 3BH

British Library Cataloguing in Publication data
A catalogue record for this book is available
from the British Library

1-85311-440-5

Typeset by Regent Typesetting, London
and printed in Great Britain by
Biddles Ltd, Guildford and King's Lynn

Contents

Contents

PART TWO: SAMPLE LITURGIES

Contents

Women

Making Liturgy

When we get together to make liturgy
   we share things,
   no hierarchies,
We are wordsmiths and story-tellers
   sculptors of images
   explorers of silences
   music makers
   singers of songs.
We move chairs
   create sacred spaces in living rooms
   set off fireworks in back gardens
   dance in cathedrals
   picnic in rain-threatening weather
   float candles in baptismal fonts.
When we get together to make liturgy
   we rejoice with the saints and the angels,
   discovering our creativity,
     being ourselves
   in the image and glory of God.

Ruth Burgess

Preface

Coming together as a group of people and worshipping a deity is an age-old expression of 'service', an act of 'doing religion', being in touch with and linked to God. In the Christian context, liturgy is the framework which lets people worship together. What started out as spontaneous celebrations, accompanying everyday as well as special experiences, developed in the life of the Church into regularized, ritualized events. Religious leaders organized worship into sets of finely-honed and patterned rituals in order to make it easier for large gatherings of people to participate. However, the rise of feminist thought in the last twenty to twenty-five years means that the praxis of expressing one's faith in set narrow and prescribed patterns no longer fulfils its role of facilitating active participation for all. Women often feel excluded from liturgies which have been created solely by men. They have taken up the arena of liturgy as participation of the people and have extended into new arenas.

The question, 'Who has the power of telling the story of God?' has become one of utmost importance. Women want to share in the creation as well as the celebration of worship, and feel the need for an inclusive liturgical experience. Liturgy is as much about sharing gifts, ideas and visions as about clothing life's events in a spiritual framework, helping individuals to cope with them.

The contributors to this book started with the question, 'When women want to celebrate a particular event, be it a Eucharist or any other occasion which gives spiritual sustenance, what *process* is required to create a liturgy?' This question of method points beyond the awareness that women rarely figure in liturgical texts, that the language tends to be non-inclusive and that symbols and images of God stress male qualities. The question of method goes beyond complaining and critiquing, it finds its strength in creating new texts with inclusive language and female images of God which focus on lived experiences.

In many places, women in tune with liberation theologies and feminist theologies have developed liturgies which are a source of strength for those who are only used to traditional forms of worship.

Thus, participating on all levels, preparing, sharing and reflecting on events, tying them into a group celebration, can be a wonderful and enriching experience. To get it right for the group, for the individuals taking part, is the remit of this book. The introductory chapters, on various topics relating to creating liturgies, lead on to a number of sample liturgies, presented not as models to be followed exactly, but to stimulate creativity. It is a 'how to' book, a tool, to encourage everybody to express their faith in ways which are meaningful to them.

Making Liturgy has grown out of women's experiences of coming together in worshipping groups in various parts of the United Kingdom. These groups are ecumenical and inter-faith and cater for women who are members of a church and for those who are not. In the book there are several references to the Roman Catholic Church, but the liturgies and contributors should not be regarded as 'catholic' in its narrow interpretation relating to that church. Conscious efforts have been made to be as inclusive as possible and to present liturgies that will suit a variety of worshipping communities.

This book is the result of many years of our trying out liturgies we have created. In different settings, for different occasions, we came together to celebrate in our particular way. And this also marked out the process of producing this book: it was a truly collaborative effort of making plans, finding the administrative and financial support, putting texts together, asking for advice, improving on the language, finding source materials, locating quotations and texts used, writing and rewriting passages, meeting and networking by phone, fax and e-mail. The talents necessary to produce such a book, the gifts brought to the task by each of us, made this a model for the whole enterprise of 'making liturgy'. So at this point I wish to say 'thank you' to everybody who took up the idea and collaborated in a very disciplined way while running busy lives with many personal, professional and charitable commitments.

Dorothea McEwan
Lent 2001

PART ONE

MAKING LITURGY

I

Worship and Liturgy: What Are They?

Worship is giving due honour and respect for something or to someone. The word 'worship' can be a noun and a verb and so it can be the activity or the action. Liturgy is the activity by which we worship God, so liturgy is an act of worship. The words 'liturgy' and 'worship' can be used interchangeably.

Worship is a public or semi-public action celebrating our search for and discovery of meaning in the mystery of life. It is the way in which a group of people give expression to their deeply held beliefs. When women and men gather to engage in the liturgical activity which we call worship, they are giving it a special time, recognizing a special significance in what they are doing. It is done not from obligation or through coercion but because there is a compelling need or wish for it. Through worship we acknowledge God's presence and importance in our lives.

Women have challenged some churches' view that only specially ordained ritual agents – priests or ministers – are authorized to initiate and lead acts of worship. In a feminist understanding of worship, all present are able to influence the whole and contribute creatively. Because each individual is important in any group, different groupings result in different acts of worship even though the basic framework is the same. Each person brings her or his history, experience and knowledge to the act of worship. Every person contributes creatively to the whole process, which is about discovering our nature and our understanding of God. In the feminist understanding, an individual may be the initiator and leader of any particular occasion of worship. Other members of the group, by their presence, empower the person for that moment. Feminist women have also challenged the patriarchal nature of many religious traditions and seek to uncover the hidden roles of women throughout religious history. They recognize and remember the contribution made by women in scripture and in the history of the Church. Women seek to use inclusive language so that God is not seen only as male, and a white male at that. Terms such as 'man', 'brothers', 'he' are not inclusive of women. Use of inclusive language demands inclusive leadership.

On an everyday level, we all engage in rituals such as birthday parties and the celebration of the special events in our lives. A great deal of thought, care and preparation can be put into these events. We are able to do what is appropriate for the occasion. We are not intimidated by the magnitude of the task. Often we will enlist the help of friends in the preparation, sharing the work. Similarly, everyone should be able to prepare and lead a liturgy. It is up to us to empower each other to be able to prepare worship that is authentic and meaningful for the participating group. The worship then truly belongs to the people. Marjorie Proctor Smith, author of *Praying with Our Eyes Open*, calls it the 'people's work'.

Acts of worship or liturgy have some basic elements. The first element is acknowledging God. The second is the desire for understanding of and learning about God. The third aspect is what that means for us and our world, especially for the powerless in it. These three elements are combined and expressed through action, word and ritual. In this way we are adding to tradition, evoking meaning, searching for just ways of acting, inspiring commitment and above all encouraging hope.

In liturgy everyday events or actions take on a special and particular significance. This enables the participants to connect and bond. For instance, in the sharing of bread we connect with each other physically as we eat the same loaf. There is something very basic or elemental about eating together. A shared meal to which everyone has contributed takes us beyond the narrow space of the individual. The ordinary act of eating, sharing food and drink, becomes endowed with symbolic meaning.

Symbols in worship are another kind of language and have many depths of meaning. They 'speak' beyond the confines of words. They engage with us at the place we are at in our understanding or belief. They enable us to grow in our understanding. The same object can have different meanings at different times, even within the same group. A symbol should only be used as long as it is helpful. Likewise, metaphors and stories can communicate truth in a gentler way than dogmatic assertions. They 'allow' our understanding and comprehension to grow organically, gradually. Jesus used parables extensively to communicate with his listeners. The revelation of God always involves more than that which is immediately obvious; but through symbols and images, metaphors and stories, and by trusting what our own life experience reveals, we can deepen and extend our understanding of and relationship with God and with the rest of creation.

On a practical level, time needs to be given to the preparation of a liturgy. It is often helpful to work in a small group, sharing ideas with one or two others. In this way, those who have experience of preparing liturgy can share their expertise and confidence with those for whom this is a new experience. Care needs to be taken in working out the framework, paying attention to how and where participants will be contributing and following through a theme with consistency. 'Keep it simple' is good advice; using too many themes or symbols will be confusing and they can be saved for another occasion. It takes time and effort to plan liturgy but it is a rewarding and renewing task.

Liturgical worship is a dynamic, symbolic, communal act. It is a place to engage in a living theology and to find a real spirituality. Through it we will both challenge and nurture our very being, our soul. Through it we will become more ourselves, more whole and more truly human. Through it we will become strong enough to work for a just world, out of life bringing hope and out of death the resurrection promise of New Life for all.

2

The Language of Symbols, Symbolic Space and Dance

'We must use what we have to invent what we desire'
(Adrienne Rich, *What is Found There: Notebooks on Poetry and Politics*)

Making liturgies means creating unique events, full of spontaneity and born out of group participation. Creative living liturgies can never become 'official' texts. They are open-ended and liable to change and develop according to the group and situation. This also applies to the use of symbols, space and to the movement and use of our bodies. Each of these elements contributes to the diversity, difference and many-layered meanings available to us when we create liturgy together.

In a world where we rely so much on words, the use of symbols, space and dance can play an important role in worship. They often speak more powerfully than words. When we make liturgy together, unbounded by set texts, structures and practices, the use of these non-verbal elements aids our imaginations to make room for God. More than this, they awaken our creativity and giftedness as human beings, whoever we are and whatever our situation.

Symbols

What do we mean by symbol? Any object can be used as a metaphor for something else. In this way the object becomes endowed with a symbolic meaning beyond its physical reality. Jesus said, 'I am the bread of life' (John 6:35). We take that to mean that just as we need bread to feed our physical bodies, we need the message of Jesus to feed our spiritual life. So the bread has taken on a symbolic meaning beyond its actual physical reality.

The Language of Symbols, Symbolic Space and Dance

The language of symbols makes an important contribution to traditional Christian worship. But when specific meanings become exclusively attached to certain symbols, their meaning becomes limited and our notions about God confined. Traditional symbols such as bread and wine provided by the gospel and the tradition of the Church, still continue to prove their communal worth. But in order to 'invent what we desire' we need to discover symbols which reflect the diversity of experience and embrace the unique spiritual path of each person. These symbols help to enlarge our imaginations and widen our insights into the nature of God.

We can re-imagine and reclaim traditional symbols in order to make them relevant to our lives and experience. For instance, candles are used widely in many church settings. Traditionally, they are set on the altar and their light referred to in words such as 'the Light of Christ'. Making our own liturgies allows us to bring that Light into a different dynamic. For example, providing an opportunity for each person to light a night-light and name, either aloud or silently, some individual or situation, is a very simple but powerful act of collaborative prayer. This can be followed by gathering the prayers together, with a simple dance, or a period of silence, and then blowing the candles out, as if to send the Light to those people and places named. An equally powerful liturgy can be created to express the darkness in our lives and in the life of the world by using extinguished candles. We can thereby reclaim the candle as a symbol of Light, which is central to Christian belief. Bringing this symbol into our liturgy, and simply experiencing for ourselves the lighting or extinguishing of the light, can help us to step into our own light, connect with each other, with the world and with God.

However, many women have needed to break away from traditional symbols in order to explore and express themselves more fully. We have discovered that symbols used in worship can speak beyond words. We can cross boundaries by the use of symbols in worship. Symbols in worship can offer many depths of meaning. Furthermore, we have needed to find other ways of speaking about God, and have discovered that symbols can be drawn from a greater breadth of experience, including our own. Writing in the *A–Z of Feminist Theology* (ed. Isherwood and McEwan) Ronwyn Goodsir Thomas expresses this well: 'Symbols arise naturally out of human experience: they cannot be artificially constructed.'

It is important, therefore, to introduce elements in worship which are based on and speak to our experience. We use objects to help our understanding. For example, a stone may take on many different meanings. A heavy stone could be used as a symbol of the heavy emotional or psychological burden we carry. It could also be used to symbolize the solidarity and steadfastness of our belief. The stone from a fruit could express that which needs to be discarded in one's life or it could mean the seed of something new to come in the future. Similarly, an empty bowl might symbolize physical hunger or it could take on the meaning of an empty or barren womb. Whatever is chosen as symbol, it needs to enhance meaning and understanding, and to come forth from those creating the liturgy of that moment.

The use of symbols, then, can take us beyond words and enable us to grow in our perceptions and understandings about life and our faith. Symbols speak for themselves. They cross between the everyday and the world of our unconscious. Exploring the sacred in ordinary everyday rituals or objects draws on our imaginations, enlarges our understanding, and deepens our faith. And there is mystery: the revelation of God always involves more than that which is immediately obvious. For example, bread and wine are common symbols in Christianity. The sharing of food relates to a basic human need. A cup of tea shared around a kitchen table is a symbol of love, hospitality and care, and relates closely to the many meals Jesus shared with different people. For many people, the embodied God hallows all the elements of life. Sharing food, whether bread and wine, milk and honey, tea and biscuits, a single bowl of rice, or a bring and share meal, becomes a eucharistic act.

The Symbolic Use of Space

It is important to consider the language of physical space in worship. Making liturgy together from a place of consensus is reflected in the way space is used in worship. The space which is set up needs to symbolize a non-hierarchical and participative process. For example, the experience of sitting in a circle where each person can see each other, is very different from that of sitting in rows one behind the other. Creating open flexible spaces by arranging the seating – perhaps with a centrepiece, hanging cloths or pictures on the walls, and paying attention to colour, smell, form, lighting and so on – all helps to provide a safe environment which we can claim for that particular time and occasion.

It is also helpful to think about the way we use space for particular themes. A liturgy which explores journeying, for example, calls for a space where people can move from one place to the next for different parts of the liturgy. Moving into a garden or space outside helps reflection on God in creation, employing our senses of touch, smell, sight, and hearing.

Examples of using space in this way are the taking of a trust walk or walking a labyrinth. For a trust walk participants divide into pairs, taking turns to be blindfolded. One person leads the other encouraging them to use their senses, touch, taste, hearing, smell and finally seeing. The labyrinth is an ancient symbol (different from a maze) in which there is one path which leads to the centre and out again. Walking a labyrinth can be used for reflection, meditation, and prayer. (Full descriptions of both these activities can be found in *Death and Renewal of Creation* by Gillian Limb, Veronica Seddon and Mairin Valdez.)

The Symbolic Use of Dance

Traditional Christian worship has made a distinction between body and soul. Feminist liturgies honour women's bodies and bodily functions. If we want to worship God with all that we are, it is vital to accept who we are, and to reclaim our bodies as God given. Here too, we need to 'use what we have to invent what we desire'. This dimension of body language is inherent in women's liturgies where the use of the body and senses and emotions can be freely expressed. We can re-discover a new sense of embodiment and a sense of connectedness. Re-discovering the senses – touch, taste and smell – adds another dimension to this sense of embodiment. For example using essential oils to massage each other's feet or hands can be healing, and life-affirming.

Many women have rediscovered their bodies through dance in worship. Circle dance is not a performance, but a participative act. Dance can be an expression of prayer, of faith and of feelings. It can be a welcome respite from words. Dance can be a meditation or a celebration, a rite of passage, an invocation. It can unite the body, mind and spirit, and transform our sense of self.

It is usual to have a centrepiece, for example a lighted candle to symbolize the Light of Christ, some flowers or an icon on a colourful piece of material or scarf, scrunched up, or perhaps arranged in a spiral.

It is always important to allow people to opt out – if they do not want to dance they might like to sit in the centre. This is an effective way of blessing one another. Everyone involved can make their contribution, dance their own dance, moving the hands or the head – we all have our limitations but we each have our own dance. As we allow people to move in and out of the group we are reminded that we are always changing, nothing is fixed – we are a flexible moving community with different needs at different times.

Circle dances are easy to learn. They are repetitive and the same steps are learned together. We give and receive to each other and to God. Dancing together should be relaxing, a letting go. It is good to encourage everyone to hold hands loosely and let their arms relax. As with a new song or chant, it is a good idea to teach dances before beginning a liturgy, so that people feel comfortable and know what to expect. At the time of the dance simply remind everyone of the steps once more. Because the steps are repetitive there is time for people to learn at their own pace. There is no right or wrong way – just make your own variations!

Circle dances can gather us together at the beginning of a liturgy, help to still us, to prepare us for worship. They can be lively or meditative. Circle dance is also an effective way to bring a liturgy together, offering up all that has been shared.

There are many simple dances – dances to chants from Taizé, to classical music, and dances from many parts of the world. Through the repeated patterns of steps we create another language and absorb the cultural language of other people, places and times without words. Drawing together in a circle constructs a powerful and immediate medium of communication. The threads of interconnection between all members are equal and interchangeable.

These different languages of symbols, symbolic space and dance can enrich our lives and nurture our faith. They can provide a connection to the transcendent, the sacred, and into the mystery of God. They also can challenge the univocal approach of traditional worship. One of our aims in this book is to encourage you, or your group, to explore and experiment with these 'different languages'. This is particularly important for individuals and groups, who, like women, do not feel they have an equal voice.

As women, we have discovered that, as Marjorie Proctor Smith puts it in *Praying with Our Eyes Open*, 'we need to evaluate traditional texts, symbols and ritual practices as to their potential for contributing to our well-being as women as well as the well-being of other oppressed peoples, rather than refer to some intrinsic authority'. Moreover, we need to 'invent what we desire' so that we can worship God with the whole of ourselves, as fully human, and with all that we are.

3

Inclusive Language in Liturgy

One important advantage of creating liturgies for worship is that the language and theme can be relevant to the needs and experience of those present. For women, often it is not only the lack of flexibility in the public worship in the Church that can be alienating but also the male-centred language: 'Pray brethren', '. . . was made man' and so on. In the Roman Catholic Church, the impact of an all-male presence at the altar (until the recent relaxation on the ban on female altar servers) also symbolizes the male-oriented structure of the institutional church, as does the distorted theology which underlies the refusal of ordination to women despite the Genesis vision that women equally as men are made in the image of God.

Some women do not feel personally alienated by referring to the community as 'men' or by male 'God-talk', but it is important in liturgy, just as in ecumenical work and for that matter in everyday life, to avoid language that is offensive to others. Further, there is evidence of the psychological effect of using exclusive language. The constant use of 'men' as the norm helps make women feel second-class citizens and reinforces their lack of self-esteem. It was some twenty years ago that the International Commission of English in the Liturgy (ICEL) pointed out the way language affects how people perceive themselves: 'Pastoral sensitivity and sound theology' should lead to use of words in liturgy and church documents that do not discourage women from playing a full part.

Sadly, little heed has been paid to this. It seems that the phrase 'men and women' was so feared that it was taken out of the original English translation of the *New Catechism*. Hence, it is all the more important that women and men openly use inclusive language as part of their prophetic witness, particularly as secular society has so largely adopted it.

There are two main aspects to inclusive language. One is the way we talk about the faith community or group with whom we are working. The other is how we picture and talk about the divine. When we read biblical passages it is helpful to use one of the inclusive language versions referred to in the Resources section and to plan ahead to ensure such a version is available. With busy lives it is easy to leave details to the last moment and then find that only a traditional, exclusive language version is to hand. It is not always easy to change pronouns and words for God as one goes along, particularly as the chosen passages for reading may be given to a member of the group who is not familiar with the process.

One of the more serious distortions (which ICEL wants to see changed) is the use of 'and was made man' (rather than 'human') in the Creed. This emphasizes the maleness rather than the humanity of Christ. However, there are a number of free-form inclusive Credos available in contemporary collections of prayers and, even better, a creed can be worked out specially for the occasion.

If the Lord's prayer is included, many people have found helpful Jim Cotter's version from his book, *Prayer at Night's Approaching*, which begins 'Eternal Spirit, Life-giver, Pain-bearer, Love-maker, Source of all that is and that shall be, Father and Mother of us all, Loving God, in whom is heaven . . .' or Lala Winkley's 'God, Lover of us all, Most Holy One, Help us to respond to you . . .' from the collection *Celebrating Women*.

The concept of God as father does not have to be banished totally, but it is necessary to counter the overwhelming use of what is only one of many divine images. This over-use has narrowed spiritual understanding in a damaging way. As it is, many people believe that because we speak of God as 'He' and 'Father', the divine must be male. It is important to widen people's understanding and to see that these are all only partial images. To use a wide variety of scriptural images enriches the understanding of and response to God. In addition to the mother image, many others are available, such as potter, healer, nurturer, as well as a lactating or pregnant woman. There are also inanimate images such as spring of water, fire, shield, or rock. Even Thomas Aquinas saw the need for many images of God, as he recognized that all are only metaphors and glimpses through a darkened glass. Part of the prophetic witness Christians are called to is to awaken awareness of this. As Sandra Schneiders wrote in her illuminating *Woman and the Word*, metaphors for God that are drawn from human experience can easily be literalized. While we are immediately aware that God is not a rock or a mother eagle, there is a great tendency to imagine that God is really a king or a father. Of course, the word 'mother' could also be taken literally, but if it is used in conjunction with other images this is less likely.

A theme of much importance in women's creative liturgy is that of relationship and connectedness – something that is hardly touched upon in most official Catholic liturgy. A valuable insight into the theological basis of this comes from feminist theological understanding of the Trinity as a relation, not of a hierarchy of Father, Son and Spirit, but of loving and equal mutuality, which is fruitfully patterned in our relationships here on earth.

Themes and ideas are part of language, for all are forms of communication. In order to express contemporary reflection on the relation of the people of God with the divine and each other, many other sources, not necessarily biblically based, have potential for developing insight. Many aspects are open for exploration and this is in itself an aspect of inclusivity, for a wide range of word, music, symbol and activity can be incorporated.

As well as the form of the liturgy created, consideration should be given to the participants – is the group reaching out to others, making it possible, by lifts in cars, for the disabled to attend? If dancing is planned, is there a way for those who have disabilities to join in? Those in wheelchairs who have the use of their upper body can be good at beating a tambourine or indeed may have greater skills on flute or other instruments. They might share in a circle dance by sitting in the centre, bearing candles. The questions relating to venue are more difficult, as places with good disabled access are often more expensive to hire, but a few strong people can often lift a wheelchair up a small flight of steps.

Inclusivity is a very broad concept and the following outline indicates some of the varied ways it can be applied to creating a relevant and living liturgy.

Possible Components of Alternative Liturgy

The items in each section are examples of the many elements from which a choice can be made. The lists are by no means exhaustive.

Introduction

- Welcome
- Naming selves
- Talking to person next to one and then introducing her/him to the group
- Telling our own stories
- Relaxation/Breathing exercises

Readings/Prayer

- Scripture (using inclusive version or adapting the text)
- Prayers, poems and prose, written by group members or from published work
- Reflection on readings (silently, or by talking in pairs or in the group)
- Meditation

Intercession and/or Penitential Rite

- Spontaneous or written
- Accompanied by: lighting candles, sowing seeds, laying down stones, putting flowers or leaves in a vase etc.

Eucharist/Agape

- Using non standard eucharistic prayers
- Traditional Agape prayers or contemporary food blessings
- Using specific food arising from readings etc., i.e. fish, bread, grapes, fruit

Using the Senses

- Making collages, weaving webs, clay modelling, drawing, painting (on a theme, expressing feelings and beliefs)

- Choosing pictures or postcards and talking about the choice

- Casting away stones or building cairns

- Walking a prepared labyrinth

Music and dance

- Singing, playing instruments, playing tapes or CDs, dancing.

- Silence

- Vocal expression of feelings, e.g. expressing opposition through humming, groaning

Body

- Centring exercises

- Holding hands, washing feet, kiss of peace, anointing with oil or blessing with water, ashes etc.

Themes

- Liturgical seasons and feasts

- Celebrations for anniversaries

- Marking rites of passage (i.e. baptism, moving house, new stage in life, death, breakdown of a relationship etc.)

- Healing and peace liturgies

- Seeking Christian wholeness, i.e. justice, friendship, images of God, relationships, wilderness, mutuality, journey, growth, creation etc.

Symbols

- Candles, water, oil, food, growing things; the Cross (including 'Christa', the female image of Christ), icons, wreaths, flowers, sowing seed, building cairns etc.

4

Creating Liturgies for Small Groups

In planning a liturgy one is planning a process which enables members of the group to worship their God together, develop their theology and spirituality, and explore how these interact with the world we live in. It is primarily a communal action. In this chapter I am looking at arrangements that are appropriate for groups of up to twenty-five people.

The aim of 'planning' a liturgy is that it should come together as a complete whole. So care needs to be given in choosing the texts, symbols, actions, music. But the most important elements are the people present. It is each person's presence and contribution that makes the occasion unique. The liturgy should therefore be structured to enable the participation of everyone present. If carefully structured, everyone will feel the need and the wish to make their special contribution. Instructions need to be clear so that everyone knows what is expected of them and so can relax. It is helpful to say that no one should feel obliged to speak or contribute if they do not wish to do so; presence is contribution. Be aware of time when planning. People get tense if they can see that the liturgy is going to over-run the allotted time by more than a few minutes.

I have found it helpful to use the elements that comprise the traditional Sunday service as a basic framework.

Possible Elements

- Gathering / Welcome / Names
- Asking for forgiveness
- The Word
- Sharing the Word
- Creed or Gloria
- Praying for special intentions

17

- Eucharist (literally 'thanksgiving')
- Blessing / Kiss of Peace

These are possible elements. Some can be left out, others can be added; the order can be rearranged. Always be flexible.

Choose the Theme

If the liturgy is for a special occasion (such as a birthday or remembering a friend who has died) there is no difficulty in choosing the theme. But if you are part of an on-going group that meets to worship together and you have taken on the task of planning, then you will want to give the theme some thought. You might wish to focus on an aspect of the liturgical year, or the season of the year, or something in the news, or a social issue. It may be that something keeps coming into your mind and so you decide to focus on that. Whatever it is, choose the theme and stick with it. (Remember that there is bound to be another occasion when you can use other ideas.)

Choose the Reading(s)

The main reading or readings will relate directly to the theme. They can be from scripture; you may choose to use poetry or prose. You may find several suitable texts but may need to leave the final decision as to which to include until later. Probably two readings will be enough. A single reading, used carefully, can be very effective. There are plenty of good resources (see the Resources section at the end of the book).

Food and Drink

Decide on the food or drink that you want to share for the eucharistic element. This may be obvious from the theme and the text. For example, if the theme is harvest, then fruits would be suitable. If the theme is hunger, then bread and water could be shared. If you are celebrating a birthday, you may wish to share a cake. If your theme is 'being in the wilderness' then you might use milk and honey, the food longed for in the desert (see Leviticus 20:24). And of course there is a long tradition of using a loaf of bread and a cup of wine.

What will Happen

Start at the beginning with 'Gathering / Welcome / Names'. One of the planners can welcome people to the liturgy and explain what is the theme and why it has been chosen. She can acknowledge her co-planner(s). Then everyone in the circle can name themselves. In naming themselves, each person becomes present and valuable. It takes very little time to go around the circle so that everyone may say their own names and immediately have a voice. It is possible to extend the introduction, by asking people to share with a neighbour some aspect of their lives or their reaction to the theme. There are always many alternative ways to begin a liturgy.

Somewhere in this opening will be a moment to light the candle (or candles) to signify Christ's presence: 'For where two or three meet in my name, I shall be there with them' (Matthew 18:20).

Sharing the word: It is important that what is read is clearly heard and you may wish everyone present to have a copy of the text. The person (or persons) who reads need not be the planner. There are various ways to process what has been heard. After a short silence, those present can be invited to share their reflections. Or you might suggest breaking into groups of two or three and taking fifteen minutes or so to reflect together, after that time coming back into the full group and sharing what has been discovered. Whatever you decide, it is important that this is not about argument or discussion but about responses. It is about each person being respected for what they wish to contribute. You might wish to incorporate some non-verbal sharing, such as drawing or making a collage. Alternatively, the drawing or collage could be made by the whole group.

Creed or Gloria: This is an optional element, but I include it to suggest a way of making communal prayer on the spot. Each person could be invited to speak out a belief that is important to them, or groups of two or three people could create a creed or gloria together, spending ten to fifteen minutes on the writing. Coming back together, each group or pair could read out their prayer.

Praying for other people / issues: It is helpful to have some gesture or action to facilitate this prayer time. Each person could light a candle (one hour night- or table-lights) as they speak, or take up a specified object or place a flower on to the centrepiece. You will find something appropriate to your theme.

Eucharist: This eucharistic sharing can be quite simple. It can consist of some appropriate words (said by one person or all together) and passing the food round the circle and probably each giving to the next person so that each 'ministers' to another. If drink if used, it can be shared in the same way.

If you are sharing bread, there are many words from scripture to use. Jesus said, 'I am the bread of life. Who comes to me will never be hungry; those who believe in me will never thirst' (John 6:35). Words from one of the feedings miracles might be chosen, or the story of the woman at the well in John 4.

Blessing and ending: Choose a blessing prayer to say together or write one for the occasion. Sometimes it is good to end with a song, or dance or a kiss of peace; sometimes ending in silence is right. However you conclude it should be appropriate to the theme.

Creating a Visual Centrepiece

It is always helpful to have something for the eyes to focus on immediately one sits down. It sets the scene and the theme and the mood. It can be as simple as a cloth and a candle. You may wish to include the food for the eucharistic element or you may keep that to one side for later. You can use objects from nature or things from your home. When the group gathers this is what they will be looking at first. Objects can be powerful symbols and aid the imagination (see 'Food and Drink' above). Having approximately the right number of chairs set out ready around the centrepiece looks inviting and extra chairs can always be added.

Using Music

The music should always be part of the integrated whole, not just 'tacked on' at the end, so you may wish to have music playing as the participants arrive. An alternative is to play some music right at the beginning of the liturgy to set the theme. If you have some singing then you may need to practise briefly before commencing the liturgy (see 'What will Happen' above).

When Things do not Go as Planned

Sometimes a particular part does not work as it was envisaged. This is not a disaster but the opportunity for learning and doing it differently next time. The most important thing is to be honest and sincere in planning and to remember that you are setting up a process to enable a group activity. The planners are not the important part of the process; it is the people present who make a liturgy.

Giving Clear Instructions

At each stage of the liturgy give clear instructions as to what is going to happen and what is needed from the participants. Don't just expect to go round the circle at each stage. (Sometimes it is helpful for the planner to start the process.) Instructions should clarify when participants can respond in random order. Be clear that they only need to speak if they wish to; some people find it very difficult to speak into a large circle, but may be perfectly at ease talking to just one other person in a pairing. If some action and words are asked for (such as voicing a prayer while adding a stone to the centrepiece) recognize that some may wish to do the action only.

Sharing Responsibility

If you are planning as a group of two or three, then always make the plan first. Only at the end decide who will take responsibility for each part. Sharing out the responsibility of each section is a good model of ministry.

5

Creating Liturgies for Large Groups

Organizing a liturgy for a large group of people can seem a daunting challenge but at the same time it can be viewed as a real opportunity to offer participants an experience of sharing in liturgy which is inclusive, and participative, one which will give them the chance to see how the whole day's experience can be taken and gathered up into worship. This gives a special significance to all that takes place during the event and acknowledges God being with us throughout.

The liturgy for a large group is often part of a conference or gathering which has an overall organizing group but it may also be a large group of family and friends celebrating or commemorating a special occasion. The liturgy planning group needs to comprise at least two and if possible three or four members who will take responsibility for the worship. This widens the creativity, enables the tasks to be shared and gives a good role model for shared ministry. This group will need to begin by exploring ideas and planning in general terms, but once the final preparations are being made, it is probably best for clear responsibility for different aspects of the work to be allocated. For example, someone needs to ensure that all the resources are in the right place at the right time, another needs to be responsible for the sound system and for the briefing of readers and speakers on its use. A checklist to help with the allocation of tasks is included at the end of this chapter. Essentially: choose a theme, keep it simple and running through the day and build on it with the resources you use. Keep the framework of the organization clear and uncomplicated.

The theme and format of larger liturgies are usually determined by the content of the gathering and it is important for the liturgy planning group to be kept fully informed about the agenda of the day so that they can be both creative and practical about the liturgy. They need to know the expectations of the event organizers and to be aware, well in advance, of any constraints imposed by the venue or background of the participants.

The purpose and the place of liturgy in the context of the day as a whole needs to be clearly determined. Some of the best experiences of liturgy are those where it is an integral part of the day, acting as a link throughout the proceedings. For example, you can start the day with the welcome and introductions and then set the theme of the day in a short, ten-minute, liturgy. At lunchtime the liturgy can briefly bring together the morning's reflections and include a blessing for the meal to be shared. The final liturgy will gather up the whole day and be both a reflection on it and an opportunity to form resolutions for future action if appropriate.

When the main worship is at the end of the day, it is vital that the timetable allows for this to be unhurried. After a busy time spent listening, thinking, meeting people and sharing, the liturgy provides a period when the day's experiences can be considered in different ways and allows for peaceful reflection, thanksgiving and celebration. Sufficient time needs to be allocated for this to happen without participants worrying about catching their transport home. It is worth remembering that contributions from participants may take longer than anticipated. It is better to allow plenty of time for the conclusion of the day and to finish earlier, then perhaps have a cup of tea for those who can stay, than to be rushed or to over-run. The organizing group also needs to allocate time for the room to be set up for the liturgy and for participants to have a short break before gathering for the final celebration.

Worship Space

The space available for liturgy can be anything from a comparatively small meeting room to a large hall or a church or chapel. If the liturgy is to be an integral part of the gathering it is usually better to stay in the space that has been used for any other plenary sessions during the day, than to move to a designated church or chapel which has not been a central meeting place. During the conference, words and experiences, pain and joy, will have been shared; it is good to use the space where this has happened, so that the liturgy can gather it all up.

If possible visit the venue before the day itself to get a 'feel' for its atmosphere and what can be done there. Identify the strengths and weaknesses of the space. Consider the seating: is it fixed or movable? Will participants be able to move around? Find out where the electrical sockets are, where you can get water, where the light switches are; see how the heating works – a noisy system may drown any quiet moments! How good is the sound system and how does it work? Always try the sound system out beforehand so that you know for yourself whether a normal speaking voice will be adequate, or if sound projection is needed. On the day, find an opportunity for those needing to use a microphone to try it out first – it gives them greater confidence and it is vital that all participants can hear all that is going on. If the system has idio-syncrasies, brief the participants about these. It is helpful if one member of the liturgy group takes responsibility for this.

Theme

The theme of a large gathering is set by the purpose of the day and the liturgy planning group will need a clear outline of what this is. If relevant, make sure that a copy of the briefing notes is sent to the speakers and, if possible, an outline of the content – some speakers submit their papers beforehand. Give yourself time to mull over the theme, jotting down any ideas. At your initial meeting, concentrate on letting the ideas flow and take them all without letting practical constraints get in the way. Many ideas may seem unrealistic or unacceptable but organizers need to be as tolerant as possible so that creativity is not stifled at this stage.

Look at all the ideas, select the one that 'feels' right and stay with this, making sure that this central theme runs through all the worship of the day. List any connected resources that come to mind immediately – think of colours, shapes, words, poetry, readings, music, dance, aromas, symbols and objects that link to the idea. Consider where worship is required in the programme and think about what type of format will fit best. Make a provisional time allowance for each part: welcoming, introducing, gathering up, readings, action, reflection and blessing. Anticipate how participants will be included, and what they can say and do.

When using music on a tape or CD, play the piece beforehand and set the tape to the place you want to begin. If you have several pieces it is often better to have separate tapes for each one so that you will have peace of mind in knowing that each is set to the correct place and that you don't have to search for the right music. Always turn the player on and off as quietly as possible and play the piece in gradually by turning the volume up. At the end turn it down gradually to silence. This avoids the otherwise abrupt beginnings and ends of the music and the 'clunk' of some music players.

Readings and Service Sheets

When you have chosen your readings:

- Decide whether they will be read from a book or will be on separate sheets for the readers.
- If they are to be on paper, print enough copies for the readers and for the liturgy group to have one each – just in case you have to 'step in' at the last minute.
- If they are to be read from books, decide who is to take the books, have the place clearly marked on the page with start and finish of the passage identified. Make photocopies for the planning group.
- Make sure readers have sight of their readings in good time.
- Be ready to support anyone who lacks confidence in reading or speaking to a large group; hold a practice if necessary.
- Give each reader a service sheet with the place for their reading clearly marked.

The service sheets need careful consideration; if every word is printed out in full, participants tend to bury their heads in the paper and read rather than listen, something which can detract from the experience. A compromise is to have the main outline on the sheet, including the reading references, so that they can be looked up afterwards. Any prayers, readings, responses or blessings which are to be said by everyone should be in a good-sized, clear print so that they can be seen and read easily. Choose the colour of paper carefully so that the print contrast is good – a brightly coloured paper may seem cheerful but it can sometimes cause print to be illegible. An appropriate border or motif can help to make the sheet look attractive and serve later as a reminder of the day.

Participation

With a large group of people it is essential that everyone feels that they are taking part and are not merely onlookers and listeners. Everyone needs to feel that they can make a contribution, if they wish to, but this cannot always be done individually if the numbers are very large. Allowing people to be vocal at the start of the day gives them a voice for the day. Build on opportunities for everyone to share. In the opening liturgy everyone could be asked to say their name aloud, to introduce themselves to those around them or to talk briefly in groups of three about their hopes for the day. When there are a number of distinctive groups present at the gathering, representatives can be asked to speak or act for each group, so that everyone feels part of the worship. After a reading, small groups, positioned near to each other, could share their thoughts on it for a couple of minutes. Personal contributions cannot always be vocal so look for opportunities to use actions and symbols to include everyone.

Ensure that the liturgy centrepiece is where everyone can see it. In a hall it may be possible to arrange chairs around the setting on the floor. In a chapel or church you can consider the use of the altar steps or tables at a suitable height.

An example of a liturgy which ensured participation took place at a Human Rights Conference. The opening liturgy started with music to invite everyone to settle and gather together around the large purple cloth laid on the floor. On this cloth was a large, beautiful, glazed blue bowl filled with water, a large candle and several small, unlit night-light candles. After the introductions the large candle was lit so that the light would be with us throughout the day and we prayed together that we would come to the living God, stand alongside the poor and resist all that offends God's justice. We then listened to a reading of Isaiah, which provided our reflection and theme for the day. One person from each of the participating groups was then asked to name their group aloud, to lay a group symbol down while briefly explaining it, and to light a candle. We ended with a few minutes of quiet reflection before listening to the speaker and moving into discussion groups.

After the discussion groups, everyone gathered together again as music was played. There was an invitation to a short, quiet reflection on the group work before someone from each group was invited to name the pain experienced in the group and to put down a word or symbol representing it. Together we prayed a short litany for justice and then asked those who so wished to put a few grains of salt into the bowl of water which represented the hurt, bitterness and pain which we now shared. Salt is also an important ingredient in bread. As we shared our hurt and pain together, so we also blessed and shared bread before we joined together for lunch.

In the afternoon participants split into different discussion and planning groups, looking at the way forward for achieving justice. The liturgy was designed to include contributions from the groups and we had asked them to produce a statement and a pledge to move forwards to achieve human rights. Again, music helped to bring people together and set the reflective mood. We prayed together that we would move from our small horizons to the vastness of God's vision; each group was invited to read the group declaration and pin it on to the prepared board behind the liturgy centrepiece. We listened again to the reading from Isaiah, reflecting quietly on this and on the symbols that had been built up through the day. On the purple cloth we now had our group symbols showing that we were united in sharing both the pain and joy of working towards human rights for everyone, and the large candle which had been burning throughout the day. The bowl of salt water represented both our tears and a healing for our wounds. The candles represented all of us, and those known to us who suffer injustice and whose voices are silenced. Our group pledges were the way in which we would move out from there to restore human rights. In conclusion, someone from each group was invited to take a lighted candle, offer it to someone else and so share the light.

It is important to ensure that a liturgy ends in a positive way. Everyone can be asked to take away one thought, feeling or action from the day; if practical a small piece of paper or card can be provided for this to be written on. The sign of peace is uniting and a concluding dance gives a joyful ending and can be used in even very large gatherings – leading out to the new way forward.

Throughout the liturgy the 'leaders' will need to be listening and watching, sensitive to how individuals are participating. The framework for such a large liturgy will be clear and well planned and although there is not the flexibility possible with smaller gatherings, experience will teach when to make changes that come about through circumstances or the nature of contributions. The advantage of having a liturgy group with more than one person leading the worship is that you can use each other's expertise, experience and skills.

At the start of the liturgy have a clear picture of what is to happen and how contributions may be made. Instructions during the liturgy need to be clear and uncomplicated but avoid endless directions that intrude on the content. Above all, ensure everyone feels part of the proceedings and is able to contribute something. Be assured that no one, except those involved in the planning, will know when something has gone wrong or is not as intended! Be creative and confident that all will be well.

Creativity always needs to be supported by good planning which helps the liturgy to run smoothly and seamlessly. The following check-list may help to indicate some of the things which need to be considered for the event. Make copies for the liturgy planning group and indicate on it who is doing what both before and on the day. And when it is all over, further suggestions can be added to the list to help in planning for the next time.

Checklist

Venue

Check:
- strengths and weaknesses of the space
- seating – fixed or movable?
- fixtures – altar, lectern etc. if in a chapel
- acoustics
- sound system
- position of electrical sockets
- position of light switches – possibility of different effects
- heating controls – warmth – noise
- availability of water
- what will be available for you to use on the day and what things you will have to bring: extension leads, plants/flowers, vases, candles, candle holders, tape/CD player
- table/altar – large/small

Goodies box

A small box to contain:
- Blu-Tack
- Sellotape
- map/drawing pins
- glue stick
- felt tip pens – different sizes
- pen/pencil
- scissors

Liturgy items

Identify what is needed for the specific liturgy:
- cloth
- backdrop/display
- readings
- service sheets
- candles/holders/matches
- flowers/plants/vases
- symbols
- artifacts
- tape/CD
- tape/CD player
- containers for water – bowl/jug
- visual images
- ribbons

6

Choosing Music for Liturgy

Music as Enabling

Music is power, and often marginalized people located in small alternative worshipping groups lack power. The task of those leading liturgies is to empower those taking part and also to harness the musical skills of those present, so that they too can share in the musical leadership. The guiding principles underlying the use of music in liturgy are that it is accessible to those present and that it reflects the theology underpinning the liturgy.

These principles can be worked out in a variety of ways. There are three ways in which we engage with music – through listening (with or without movement), through performing someone else's pieces and by creating pieces for ourselves. It will enhance liturgies if participants are empowered to encounter music through each of these doorways. Sadly, the less confident that people feel, the more restricted they are likely to be in the way in which music is used or they may even avoid it altogether. If we omit music, we deprive liturgy of one of the most profound ways of creating a unity out of the worshipping group and also of an art form that often reaches to the deepest parts of our personalities, especially our emotions and feelings.

Inclusive Language

Music is often allied with language. Hildegard of Bingen writes:

> The words of a hymn represent the body, while the melody represents the soul. Words represent humanity, and melody represents divinity. Thus in a beautiful hymn, in which words and melody are perfectly

matched, body and soul, humanity and divinity, are brought into unity. (*Scivias* 3.13.1)

As the music fuses with the words in this close way, it is important that the words reflect the humanity of the people present. Here we encounter the issue of inclusive language. This has three aspects.

First of all it involves finding non-male words to describe people and (more significant in the hymn traditions) the use of the word human and not the word 'man' as a generic term for human beings. This is an important issue when dealing with hymns from the past. It is interesting to see how liturgical groups deal with this problem. Whereas large conferences, based on feminist principles and drawing on a wide variety of liturgical traditions, do use traditional material (sometimes unchanged), the smaller groups tend not to. Some groups dislike the use of hymns at all, seeing them as representing a male tradition which they perceive as too cerebral. This often works against women hymn-writers using traditional structures and also male writers exploring new images of God.

The metrical constraints of hymnody make changing traditional hymns quite difficult. In fact, it is probably true to say that the past needs to be left as it is and new material should be written. In general, people don't notice the presence of inclusive language. So to change 'Good Christian men, rejoice and sing', is more contentious than a new hymn using 'all' or 'human beings' instead of the non-inclusive 'men'.

The second aspect is the need for a female divine or at least a God who embraces all aspects of gender. When we extend inclusive language to the divine we encounter more problems. There is a tradition of Marian hymns where Mary is very close to divine. To use non-gendered words like friend, companion, and healer is one solution – the truly inclusive one. There is, however, a need for female images for God to balance the two thousand-year-old tradition of male names. For example, Janet Wootton's hymn 'Dear Mother God' from *Reflecting Praise* begins 'Dear Mother God, your wings are warm about us'.

A third aspect is the absence of a large body of material by women. Although there is much new verbal material by women there is a lot less music. When Janet Wootton and I edited the collection *Reflecting Praise* we wrote the following Preface:

There exists a great wealth of women's creativity as composers and poets from every generation. Much of this is only now being redis-covered, as women reclaim their own history . . . Preference has been given to pieces that have women as author, translator, composer, or arranger, or which tell the stories of women . . . All hymns use inclu-sive language for humans. A number use female or inclusive images when referring to God, many exploring new or newly reclaimed images . . . Most exciting of all, new writers continue to spring up in the field of inclusive language, broadening its scope, and introducing the idea to wider audiences.

Despite such collections, women's material is often far less easily acces-sible than material by men. It is important that this problem is addressed.

Music Types

The first thing to do in choosing music is to decide what sort of music is appropriate for the nature and mood of the liturgy. There is a wide variety of music to choose from (by men and women) ranging from simple repetitive chants to traditional hymns. This is the introduction to the liturgy group *Women Included*, prepared by the St Hilda Com-munity:

> We use traditional hymns and carols, Taizé chants, and sometimes other chants e.g. Peruvian taught us by members. We are beginning to think about making up dances to music we particularly enjoy, but have not got very far in writing our own hymns.

Chants: These are very useful because they are easily learned and often require no printed sheets. They also enhance meditative activities well and can be sung while dancing or walking. Taizé chants are very popu-lar but there are many others around, from newly composed ones for special occasions to those from traditions like the Native American. They are also the easiest place to start creating your own material. You can use existing tunes like 'Frère Jacques' or generate simple tunes as well. Chants can be very effective when used as responses to prayers or when repeated while looking at a mandala or a central display of some kind. Candles and incense sticks add atmosphere to such meditations.

Songs (with or without a chorus): A wide selection of songs is available, ranging from those from the worship song tradition such as can be found in the popular song books *Songs and Hymns of Fellowship* and *Sounds of Living Waters*, to those of a more folksong type, as in the material from the Iona Community. Some are available in recorded form and are best learned by simply joining in. Songs with a chorus are easiest and do not require printed sheets.

Hymns: To use hymns with a number of verses you need printed sheets. Hymns, in general, are in traditional metres and the advantage of this is that you can use well-known tunes for new words. This is by far the easiest way to introduce new words. New tunes are more complex and usually need a more experienced musician in the group. Having someone in the group who plays a keyboard instrument is particularly useful for hymnody.

Music for dancing: Circle dancing is increasingly popular. It is best included when there is someone present who has experience in this area. Sometimes the group sings while dancing, in which case the song needs to be one that can be sung from memory. More often the dances are danced to recorded music. It is then important that the tape or CD is set at the right place before the liturgy begins.

Music for listening: Music can be used to set mood and atmosphere. The style and nature of the music depends on the taste of the group. Romantic orchestral music is very popular, as is unaccompanied music for flute or Celtic harp. Appropriate music can also be used to accompany readings or as a backdrop to intercessory prayers.

Improvising: The repetitive chants can be used as the basis of improvisation. While the chant is repeated by the group, individuals can be encouraged to improvise petitions or statements over it. This does require the presence of someone who has the confidence to lead and to encourage such activities.

A simpler option is to set up a group hum as the expression of group solidarity, strength and support. Humming any note that each person finds easy creates a beautiful container of sound. People sitting inside a humming circle can feel held and warmed. Prayers can be uttered over the hum or people can improvise cries and screams or laments over this supportive musical carpet. This is a very powerful way of creating a group atmosphere.

Some Characteristics of Music in Alternative Liturgies

The following points have been drawn from alternative liturgy groups that are now meeting regularly:

Embodied approaches to music-making include movement of some kind. Circle dances are often tailor-made to fit the age and experience of the group. There is also a great reliance on singing rather than on instrumental traditions. The body is accepted as it is, rather than as something that requires extending by means of technology (musical instruments).

Interconnectedness of God with her creation is reflected in the carefully planned relationship of the music to the overall context. Songs are often recreated each time to fit the situation. Groups seldom have hymnbooks of the traditional kind but more often a bank of material that is reworked. Much of the material is ephemeral. Some of the liturgies take place out of doors to reinforce the connection with the natural world, or centre around material taken from nature. There is a connection between the symbolism of the music and the visual/tactile images.

Cyclical, curving forms like repetitive chants are very popular – often more so than the more linear traditional hymn. Material is used with meditative rather than didactic intention. Shared forms of working in which musicians collaborate with one another, and oral forms of transmission, like folk traditions, are favoured. The absence of an experienced musician in many of these groups often results in the pooling of resources to make music happen. Sometimes groups explore a variety of sounds such as sighing or groaning or screaming.

There is an emphasis on sharing leadership and musical roles. This is the musical equivalent of the priesthood of all believers. There is stress on the accessibility of the music to everyone present, on democracy and participation rather than excellence.

Using Instruments

The instruments used often have to be portable because of the location of the meetings in houses or out of doors. Many groups sing unaccompanied or use a guitar or piano if available. In chanting, a drum is sometimes used. This not only offers a challenge to a traditionally male activity, but also reclaims pre-Christian traditions in which drums were central. For many centuries the use of drums in Christian worship was suppressed because of these pre-Christian traditions. The drum represents power and those who control the drums often have control of the power. In workshops many women tell the story of always having wanted to play the drums but never getting them because the boys shouted louder and the teachers wanted to keep them quiet.

The organ may be seen as replacing the drum in mainstream churches as the liturgical power instrument. Women can be quite resistant to using an organ in liturgies, probably because of its association with male value systems and men in positions of power.

Softer instruments such as flutes and recorders are often favoured and there is evidence of resistance to more powerful instruments like the brass, which again appear to have associations with male triumphalism. This reflects a wider issue concerning the character of many of the liturgies that focus on softness, gentleness, vulnerability, grief and suffering, in contrast to some more powerful women's religious traditions such as those from Africa.

A Musical Liturgy

So what might a liturgy based on music look like? This is a suggestion only:

Entry: People come into a meditative atmosphere with candles and flowers and incense and music by Hildegard playing. They focus on the music and the visual symbols.

Centring chant: Sing a chant like 'Come Holy Spirit' several times meditatively to enable them to centre, accompanied by a singing bowl (a bowl from Eastern traditions which involved a stick being pulled round its rim to produce a ringing tone – like rubbing a wine glass).

Introductions: Each person sings or chants their name rhythmically with the character they wish to communicate about their present mood.

A narrative song: A member of the group sings a song – possibly of a thought-provoking nature such as 'The Tambourine Woman'. Discussion in groups follows it on the themes raised in the song or personal circumstances related to it. Their thoughts are shared with the group, perhaps even sung.

Confession: The whole group hums any note they find easy to create a humming base for the speech. Over this people say what aspect of their lives they would like to change.

Affirmation: All sing an affirming song like 'Here I am, Lord'.

Intercessions: Candles are lit while people speak their requests and each is followed by the Taizé chant, 'O Lord, hear our prayer'.

New Life: Someone talks about a piece of music or a song that they have found particularly helpful – sharing it by singing it or by playing it on an instrument or in recorded form.

Conclusion: A circle dance or a gesture dance like 'May the blessing of light be on you'.

Summary

The music of the smaller liturgy groups functioning at present does to some extent reflect the insights of feminist theologians. Less experienced worship leaders, in general, feel more confident with words than music. There is a great deal of work to be done to empower a greater range of people musically in all roles, both in leading singing, playing instruments of various kinds and, importantly, in the area of composing. People using music for listening still also use the standard repertoire of male composers. We need to work hard to make women aware of orchestral pieces by such composers as Clara Schumann and Fanny Mendelssohn-Hensel. It is important that material by women becomes more widely known, that an increasing number of people develop the skills necessary to lead musical activities and that further exploration of improvisation in worship takes place. In pursuing these aims we can make the music of worship a true reflection of a wider and more inclusive vision of God.

7

Creating Common Ground:
Taking Liturgy to the Streets

Why Take a Cause on to the Street?

Liturgy can be a way of challenging the status quo. If this challenge is addressed to the institutional Church, it may be impossible to use the church space. Reform movements, especially in the Roman Catholic Church today, are conscious that the official Church seems to have lost touch with the gospel values of unconditional love, inclusive non-judgmental compassion and reconciliation, and attention to global social justice issues. Many committed Christians want to do something: they want to make a public statement and can no longer remain silent. An effective way to do this is by creating liturgies of witness.

Liturgy as Witness

Establishment events such as Remembrance Days are occasions when people take to the streets, but when people gather to speak out, to name a wrong and witness their commitment to righting that wrong, deeper emotions can often be present. Witnessing is seen everywhere. The Tiananmen Square massacre in China is remembered by groups of people congregating there. The school children of Soweto in South Africa are remembered with a most impressive community complex named after Henry Peterson; he was the first child to be shot dead on that peaceful walk to the education office requesting that they not be forced to take all their lessons in the Afrikaans language, something which was badly holding up their progress. The photo of the twelve-year-old's blood-soaked dead body being carried by his young friend did untold damage around the world to the government exclusively made up of white Afrikaners, who promoted apartheid as the God-given natural order. The 'disappeared' in Latin America are remembered by groups like the 'Mad Women', the mothers who walk round and round the Plaza de Mayo in Buenos Aires in Argentina, relentlessly seeking information about their loved ones. Ridiculed as mad, they give us much strength with their perseverance and courage. The slaughter of Palestinian refugees and the killings perpetrated by those from differing religious traditions cannot be forgotten. The particularly appalling strategy of using rape as a wages of war, practised recently by officially 'Christian' members of the Serb Army on Bosnian Muslim women, must also be remembered. We are driven to make this witness as part of our commitment to work for justice.

The Significance of Place

We can only go to a place where mutual presence and toleration are accepted. So often the only place where those with no representation are able to express their opinion is that literally common ground, the street. Of course in ruthless, totalitarian societies there can be horrible consequences, such as in Tiananmen Square, but sometimes a greater, deeper understanding can become manifest in the clarity of the symbolic language, as with the Black Consciousness March filling the streets of the US capital with a peaceful gathering of thousands of Afro-Americans calling for their human rights. The Veterans of Vietnam hobbling down Pennsylvania Avenue on their crutches or in their wheelchairs made a powerful statement about the futility and long-term damage of war and surely changed public opinion. Rosa Parks' simple action of sitting in a seat in the part of the bus stipulated for whites only, too weary after her long day's work to stand any more, was an icon which made visible how all humanity deserves equal respect.

The way in which women have learnt to create such liturgies can be compared to the way the political prisoners on Robben Island, South Africa, learned to share their skills and knowledge hidden from the eyes of the authority. We have been educating ourselves just as they were educating themselves, accompanied by a gentle passing on of insights which has encouraged others to grow in confidence. In the Catholic Women's Network, for instance, several of whose liturgies feature in this book, it was the tradition for three people to organize each event, with one of them then being part of the group preparing the next event. Thus skills are passed on in the most creative way possible, with respect for others and the encouragement for them to learn to listen to their own inspiration.

London Liturgies of Witness

For some years I have been involved in devising street liturgies in London for various occasions. Before the General Election of 1997 many of us felt we had to gather outside the Houses of Parliament, to pray a more humane government into power. Using an old World War One gun-box covered with blossom as our soap-box, speeches were made on the issues we felt must be addressed by the new government: housing, the arms trade, poverty, Third World debt, and women's issues, particularly domestic violence. Each speaker took a prepared piece to build into a large cross, symbolic of the pain which good government has the responsibility to alleviate. Finally we all turned our cross through forty-five degrees. It resembled the mark used on ballot papers.

Our Good Friday liturgies are often very special. They have been an alternative women's expression of suffering and death, as experienced by so many women all over the world. We have made our own Stations of the Cross by visiting statues of women all over London. At the statue of suffragette Emily Pankhurst, situated between Parliament, the seat of temporal power, and Westminster Abbey, seat of religious power, we pause to think of those suffering under corrupt political and religious systems. We move on to Boadicea, on the north side of Westminster Bridge, forced to take up arms to defend her people. We pray for those women caught up in wars, most often as pawns, and for the children too, brutally forced into the killing frenzy. We have remembered our black sisters at Cleopatra's Needle, the obelisk brought from Egypt by British troops. On another occasion we have met under the Epstein statue of the Virgin and Child in Cavendish Square, the only statue of Mary in a public place in London. We have prayed using the Rosary under the guns of the Imperial War Museum. We have stopped on many of the River Thames bridges to meditate on our role as bridge-builders. In this way we claim the street, we try to honour our foremothers and give witness of our conviction.

First Wednesday Vigils and Women Walking

Each first Wednesday of every month we keep a vigil outside Westminster Cathedral to protest against women's exclusion from ordination in the Roman Catholic Church. We meet on the piazza in front of the Cathedral, at 6 p.m. in the evening. A different person contributes the prayers each month, choosing the theme, which is often topical or fitting in with the liturgical year. We pray, sing, read out, share stories and rituals such as anointing with oils, we walk in a circle with our purple scarves placed as stoles around our necks and carry beautifully made banners clearly naming our concern. This we do with all the persistence we can muster for one hour. Every month since March 1992, there has been a regular presence at that time in that place.

We have also found that there are other occasions which compel us to do something. When someone has been punished by excommunication for speaking out on our behalf, for instance, or on Maundy Thursday, when the male clergy are renewing their priestly vows inside the Cathedral – a celebration of exclusivity if ever there was one – we feel we want to celebrate our priesthood too. Following biblical example we regularly share a 'communion'. We have often laid our hands on the cold stone of the cathedral wall as a symbolic way of bringing healing.

Our many and various activities are about building visibility. Our concerns are being witnessed by many: those going in and out of the cathedral, those who live on the piazza, the homeless, those residents who live nearby, the many shoppers and the commuters rushing home. We are witnessing to our conviction that the metaphor for the sexism practised in the particular institution of the Roman Catholic Church, embodied in the theology and practice of women's exclusion from the ordained priesthood, be looked at again and discussed, not banned as a forbidden subject and all debate silenced.

Welcoming, inclusive liturgical gatherings that celebrate the common good of our common humanity on our common ground – these provide glimpses into what the future could be. We share our gifts, our histories, our experiences, our insights and understandings. If an evil system like apartheid can be overturned, other injustices can be made to cease. No membership or payment is required to participate, nor is there exclusion of anyone on any grounds; all is held in common. Our common humanity respects each person as equally imaging our God; the one request, asked of all people of faith and none, is that we love one another.

Points to Keep in Mind When Organizing Street Liturgies

- Do not go out looking for a cause, the cause comes to you. Where something is wrong, there is a reason for doing something about it. You either pick it up and run with it to win or give it up.
- Respect your instincts and inspiration; something is pushing you to go.
- Use preparation well, gather information, gain knowledge, study, reflect, and argue the pros and cons.
- Make a decision whether to pursue one single issue or a number of related issues. Be focused.
- See the personal issue in the wider political/religious/social context.
- Enquire whether there is a movement already engaged in this particular cause. If so, work with it, avoiding duplication.
- If you feel this 'witnessing' is too big a burden, drop it or find support; do not try to go it alone.
- Most unjust activities are linked: poverty, racism, and sexism. Learn to see the connections.
- Gather a group, plan with the group your activities and effective strategies.
- Check with others the focus of your action. Trust other people's judgment, respect their experiences.
- There is a moment when you realize you have no other alternative but to go out on the street; it is a frightening moment, but you have the conviction there is no other way left to pursue.
- Be aware that you are doing the liturgies as much for yourselves as for anybody else. Action helps activists to feel energized – there is nothing wrong with doing liturgies. However, being outside means that they are not exclusive and anyone may join in.
- If you want to involve the media, you must learn beforehand how to deal with them.
- Consider the timing. The right time, 'kairos', is of crucial value for success.
- Consider the place, the space, and the appropriateness of the surroundings.

- Placards, clearly printed with a neat, short slogan, posters, banners, all have a great impact to advertise the event, the group, and the cause.
- A mark of identification is helpful. Ideas and inspiration can come from the purple scarves/stoles of the Catholic Women's Ordination movement that are used now by the whole international movement Women's Ordination Worldwide (WOW). Ideas and inspiration can come from anywhere, but symbolism must be appropriate. The purple scarf/stole symbolizes grief for the lost gifts of so many women who have been ignored and excluded by the institutional Church.
- One event will not be enough. Witnessing events need to be repeated again and again; you need dedication, perseverance and persistence.
- Finally, the question of results or success: can you cope with a situation which is open-ended, where success is not guaranteed? This is the hard question and it is a reason for working with a group and not on your own. So make sure that there are occasions for laughter, for the tears will undoubtedly come. This is a lesson we learnt from the women of Soweto who, despite the years of struggle, taught us to dance and sing for joy. We thank them.

8

Liturgy's Powerful Effects

'Behold I make all things new': these words have never been truer than when applied to the search for a spirituality and theology that nurtures the innermost part of our beings. It is in making liturgy together that all our desires can be transformed and gradually realized, not only for ourselves, but for others as well.

I have been involved with women's ecumenical liturgical groups over the past fifteen years. These groups have included regular small groups of women as well as very large gatherings of over a thousand, as at the First European Women's Synod in Gmunden, Austria in 1996 and the End of the Decade on Women of the World Council of Churches (WCC), in Harare in 1998. From these experiences I offer the following theological reflections on the effects of making liturgy.

Liberation theology has popularized the process of action/reflection/action, but I prefer to speak in terms of awakening/reflection/action, because I believe these words crystallize the process out of which women's theology emerges. The symbolic process of liturgy-making has 'awakened' in women a deep sense of the inherited 'dualism' between body and soul, as if they were distinct entities, and the false complacency produced by the concept of complementarity between the sexes. The scriptural claim that humans are the 'temples of Jesus Christ' has not been a major experience for women. However, when women find God in themselves, a transformation begins to occur in their self-understanding. They become a nurturing, healing, if challenging, presence for others. In fact they become icons of change.

The use of the whole body in worshipping the God within – 'embodiment' in theological terms – , rather than a God far removed from us, evokes reflection on the misuse of women's bodies, and the philosophical and theological flaws in the formation of Christian theology.

43

The origin of what is known as 'dualism' has been traced back to the Greek philosopher Aristotle. According to Aristotle, the central way of understanding the differences between men and women was that only the free adult male qualified as a full person, because only he possessed the capacity to reason. Women were thought to be irrational and passive. To be born female was considered the most common kind of deformity.

This thought was taken into the fledgling Christian tradition and embedded in the theology of the Fathers of the Church. It was articulated clearly and almost unashamedly in the theology of Thomas Aquinas, who described women as 'misbegotten males'. Dualism gradually became an integral part of all philosophy and theology; women were considered to signify the bodily function while men represented the higher intellectual part of life. Women were seen as prone to their emotions and their role was to be passive to the wishes of men in all spheres of life.

The accumulation of such thought led to widespread consensus – still prevalent in some cultures – that women are born to complement the bodily needs of the male. Or, as one seventeenth-century cleric put it, they are 'vessels for use'. Women have been, and still are, perceived as people who do not have special gifts of their own, a right to a life of their own or, in the words of Virginia Woolf, a 'right to a room of their own'. A man's God-given right to beat his wife was once a part of the Canon Law of the Roman Catholic Church. And in that church, in particular, the treatment of women as second-rate human beings has been and still is elevated to the authority of law and can be found within Papal Encyclicals. These inherited concepts of woman have led to women being treated as non-persons.

This may sound exaggerated, but both academic research and the personal experiences of women clearly support these findings. Aruna Gnanadason, as part of her work for the WCC in the Decade on Women, 1988–98, has researched the psychological and theological impact of these attitudes which seemed to her to be so entrenched as to be inherited. One outcome of such an inheritance of disregard is mirrored in the most recent development, that of the modern slave trade, trafficking in women for prostitution, mainly women from the poorer countries of Eastern Europe. To make the connections between the treatment of women and the theology we have inherited is unfortunately the first and most crucial step necessary to begin revisioning the Christian tradition from the perspective of the powerless. The process of healing humankind from the profound sicknesses of sexism and racism is primarily dependent on women's anger and passion for justice being channelled into fruitful sources for change.

This process of awakening is a risk. It does not lead all women to stay within their religious traditions and this is reflected in women's theological and liturgical groups. Some members leave the Church, others change their denominations, while others feel attracted to the Goddess movement. However, for the majority of women in the poorer areas of the world these options are not available. To be able to choose your religion is a luxury of the western world.

Where women are confined by their poverty, they stay within their traditions, trying to improve conditions, if at all possible. However, women everywhere realize more and more that 'the personal is political'. What they have experienced in their lives has to be brought to public gaze if change is ever to occur. The American black slave community understood well the meaning of this phrase, and gave it voice in the coded Negro Spirituals of their time. Without these songs of protest, the political action of the civil rights movement would have been severely weakened or might not ever have come about. The oppressed had to speak out against their oppressors. That is the way too in the women's movement. Silence is no longer possible.

Similarly, the shared liturgical expression of women is both personal and communal. Prayer, song, dance and thought unite women of all countries and continents. They know that two thousand years and more of injustices against women will not be undone in a single generation. But a spirituality and theology, which uses new words and images of God and using healing rituals for the worst forms of abuse, can be created out of shared prayer and liturgy. Women are making the connections with their past from which a passion for justice arises. This inevitably leads to an awakening to the need for and action for change. Hope springs from these shared liturgical experiences, so that women can together dream and envision a new future where they are at last given their full God-given human dignity. Liturgy is new theology in the making; theology is new liturgy in the making.

So liturgy can serve as the basic grounding for change and lead to a spiritual theology of protest that develops from increased awareness and the stirring of consciences; liturgical experience channels the emotions kindled, and transforms them into action. This leads to further awakening, protest, action, and so the cycle is continually and creatively repeated.

It is from these foundations that the women's theological movement has begun to challenge the misogynist and patriarchal nature of much of our inherited theology. Before the middle of the last century no one would have thought of talking about 'women's theology', but now it is a fast growing part of the theological enterprise. Women affirm the belief that all experience of God comes through the body. This approach transforms and returns theology to the wholeness of the 'spiritual theology' of the early Church, but this time the experience of women has a central place. Hence, all theology begins and ends in communal liturgical expression, personal contemplative prayer and social action for justice. If any of these elements are missing, theology is sterile. Theology is the final act. For women, the creation of liturgy, therefore, is a vital expression of the action of a just God in their lives. It is a natural form of protest at the male bias in inherited liturgical expression. This is clear from the many prayers and songs that women use in their worship. Prayerful reflection is mirrored in the actions for justice which follow this realization and all culminate in a renewed holistic, life-giving, nurturing, theology.

Many schools of feminist theology are developing, and there will never be one sole discourse as before. In reaction to the inherited dualism of body and soul, new ways of theological thinking have developed. We now speak of 'body theology' and 'eco-feminism', terms that reflect a recognition that the old dualism had shaped ways of speaking not only about humanity, but about nature as well. Some women theologians are revisionists, others describe themselves as post-Christian, while still others find their spiritual nurture in the Goddess movement, or as spiritual feminists. Difference is the essence of women's theology.

One of the major differences between women's theology and all others is the claim that reflection on women's experience is the bedrock of all women's theology. This approach is known as the inductive method of theology because it is drawn from experience. It stands in contrast to the main male approach of the past, the deductive approach, which starts from given ideas and principles. The difference in methodology which arises from this approach can cause problems for women who are studying theology, and who find it very difficult to assimilate the traditional theological diet they are given. If they wish to substitute their own ideas, and even those of other women theologians, it is often not acceptable. The Women's Theological Centre in Boston, USA, was set up in the 1980s for the purpose of providing a breathing space for women studying theology, and to develop a new way of studying theology, including the essential ingredients – awakening/reflection/action – rather than a purely academic approach. One person who attended this Centre was the Korean theologian Chung Hyun Kyung, who danced at the Assembly of the World Council of Churches in Australia in 1994. Her remarks to her American professors after gaining her doctorate are noteworthy: 'I have learnt to speak your language, now you must learn to speak mine'. And her response to their limited understanding of theology was to write her own moving book, *Struggle to be the Sun Again*. Many other women from developing countries are also writing rich theologies from their own contexts and perspectives. In the process they are correcting the racist bias which they find in white women's theology. The famous cry 'the personal is political' now resonates in the women's movement and finds its Christian identity in the powerful process of liturgy-making among women.

This spirituality for the 'long haul', filled with hope which underpins the theological cycle of awakening/protest/awakening, is summed up in words by Carolyn McDade:

> The rest of our lives, my sisters, must be lived
> in the best of struggles, the best of struggles,
> in the best of struggles, our lives must be lived.

> If the road should disappear
> We'll shake the dust from our feet
> And walk on.

> If the road shall disappear
> We'll shake the dust from our feet
> And walk on.

(*Womancenter*, Plainville, 1989)

All aspects of these changing attitudes towards orthodox religion are reflected in the many women's groups that meet regularly to share liturgies and discuss theologically. It is an exciting enterprise.

PART TWO

SAMPLE LITURGIES

Introduction

The section which follows presents the adapted texts of a number of liturgies which have been used by small groups made up of people belonging to a range of Christian denominations or to none. The source of each liturgy is given in the Acknowledgments that follow the Resources section. The resources listed give details of the places where the readings, prayers, songs and poems that were used can be found, and from which alternative selections can be made. These liturgies are provided as **examples** rather than **models** – it is much better to devise your own liturgies, based on the needs of your own group, and to use readings which you find evocative, than to rely on someone else's expertise.

Each liturgy is prefaced by some details about the elements used and, where relevant, its original setting and purpose. In the account of the actions performed, the past tense has been used in order to emphasize that the liturgy described should be used to provide ideas which might be adapted to suit other groups.

The variety of sources and occasions means that these liturgies follow a range of different formats, and the features identified in the chapter on 'Creating Liturgies for Small Groups' (Gathering/Welcome/Names; Asking for forgiveness; The Word; Sharing the Word; Creed or Gloria; Praying for special intentions; Eucharist; Blessing/Kiss of Peace) are not uniformly present. Nevertheless, many of them do occur, while the summaries given do not always do justice to the length of time spent on opening and closing ceremonies, or the sections where actions predominated over words. In the liturgies presented below, the 'Gathering/ Welcome/Names' aspect is referred to as 'Introduction'; 'The Word' occurs in the 'Readings'; 'Sharing the Word' is generally present in the discussions which varied between pairs, small groups, and the whole group; while the 'Eucharist', literally 'Thanksgiving', is most frequently articulated in the sharing of food, which often took the form of bread or fruit, and drink (usually water or wine). Many of the liturgies suggest an 'Introduction'; this may take the form of a few words of welcome or description, an aspect which is likely to need some preparatory thought from one of the participants.

The liturgies have been divided into three categories: those which relate to seasons of the church or calendar year; those on themes such as justice or change; and those which are particularly, in one instance exclusively, linked with women, either as our foremothers or in relation to the stages of human life. It may be of interest to observe that no Christmas liturgy as such is included. This results from the fact that the members of women's groups are likely to be celebrating Christmas with their own families; the fact that there is an Advent liturgy may partly compensate for this, as well as suggesting that women find this season of preparation resonates with their personal spirituality.

Arrangements

In most instances, these liturgies originally took place with participants sitting in a circle, although occasions when they broke up into smaller groups, or took part in some form of movement, are clearly indicated. It is generally convenient to have a table or some other central object as a focus; the table could be covered with an attractive cloth with a candle or flowers as a centrepiece.

Elements

This term is used to indicate the material objects which were used when the liturgy originally took place; examples which occur frequently are bread, fruit, oil, flowers, etc. This word is intended to suggest the sacramental nature of the objects concerned, symbolizing much of the meaning conveyed. In using the liturgies, feel free to make your own choice of objects, remembering that such things can have a very strong symbolic significance, often conveying their meaning more effectively than words.

Readings

Use of a Bible has been assumed in what follows, so scripture readings have not been given in full. It is recommended that scriptures be read in an inclusive language version. Reference is also made to other readings which were used at the time, and to various books of which details will be given in the Resources section. These books are a valuable resource which groups would find it very helpful to possess. But it is important to make the liturgy your own by choosing your own readings. Those supplied below should be taken merely as illustrative.

In some instances, readings were used as introductions, but a few brief words about the theme of the liturgy may be equally appropriate; alternatively liturgies may begin with a song or action. It is usual to share the readings between several participants, who should be given a chance to look at the text before reading it to the group.

Participation

In the texts which follow, the use of **bold** type indicates that everyone present should join in the prayer. In many of the liturgies, reference is made to psalms or prayers being read antiphonally. This mode, much used in monastic settings, demands that participants be divided into two groups, usually labelled A and B, who alternate in their readings. *Italics* are used to denote actions which took place in the original liturgy. This is intended as an indication of what seemed appropriate to the creators of that liturgy, and those preparing their own liturgies should use their own judgement about the actions that will best suit their own situations.

When a liturgy concludes in a 'Blessing', participants may like to use their own words or others with which they are familiar, such as: 'The grace of our Lord Jesus Christ, the love of God and the fellowship of the Holy Spirit be with us now and always.'

Music and Dance

In some instances, actual instruments were played during these liturgies, but the possibility of doing this depends on the resources of the group. Songs do not need to be accompanied, and generally any familiar tune which fits the words may be used. Where dancing is suggested, participants may like to sing or hum if instrumental accompaniment is not available. Silence may often be just as appropriate as music. As with the readings, mention is often made to songs that were used when these liturgies took place. When no specific title is mentioned, or if you find it difficult to obtain the one mentioned, you should feel free to make your own choice. Some of the hymns and songs are readily available in hymn and song books. Where details of this are known these are included. For those without tunes identified see if they fit to a tune familiar to your group or make up a new tune and so add to the resources available. Remember too that many suitable songs and tunes are listed in the Music part of the Resources section which follows the Liturgies.

In many instances, appropriate atmospheric music on tape or CD possessed by members of the group will help create the desired background. Taizé chants (see the Resources section for details) will often provide a suitable atmosphere. More specific suggestions about the use of music are to be found in the chapter in this book by June Boyce-Tillman (Chapter 6). Advice about the use of dance and, in particular, the significance of the 'circle dance' can be found in the chapter by Gillian Limb (Chapter 2).

Enactment

When these liturgies were originally enacted, there was frequently some form of action appropriate to the words, symbols and themes; this has generally been indicated by the use of italics.

SEASONS

Advent: Advent Wreath

This Advent liturgy makes use of the traditional elements associated with the season, such as candles and green foliage, and culminates in a sharing of bread and wine.

Elements

> Advent wreath and four candles
> Chains of an evergreen plant, such as ivy
> Bread and wine

Introduction

A few words were spoken about different sorts of 'advent'.
We may want to remember the promises of Christ's second coming, or think about the different ways in which God comes to each individual. Alternatively, we may want to think about types of coming in everyday life, from the expectations of pregnancy to the visits of long-awaited friends.

The first candle was lit.

Reading

The Looking
> You keep us looking.
> You, the God of all space,
> want us to look in the right and wrong places

for signs of hope,
for people who are without hope,
for visions of a better world which will appear
among the disappointments of the world we know.

All   **So thank you for the looking time.**

Song

On an Advent theme
(*In Praise of All Encircling Love*, Vol. 1)

Prayer

Isaiah 35 and Micah 4:1–4 (Rejoice!)
(*The passages may be read antiphonally.*)

The second candle was lit.

Reading

The Keeping
You keep us
through hard questions with no easy answers;
through failing where we hoped to succeed
and making an impact when we felt we were useless;
through the patience and the dreams and the love of others;
and through Jesus Christ and his Spirit
you keep us.

All   **So thank you for the keeping time.**

Discussion (in pairs or larger groupings)

What does Advent, as a time of waiting and looking forward, mean to us personally?

Song

'Embracing the darkness'
(*In Praise of All Encircling Love*, Vol. 2)

The third candle was lit.

Reading

The Waiting

> You keep us waiting,
> you the God of all time,
> want us to wait for the right time in which to discover
> who we are, where we must go,
> who will be with us, and what we must do.

All   **So thank you for the waiting time.**

Prayer

'For the darkness of waiting'

(Janet Morley in *All Desires Known*, adapted from Psalm 139 and Romans 8:18–25 – Life through the Spirit)

The fourth candle was lit.

All stood in a circle, linked by a chain of vegetation, such as ivy, singing.

Song

> Weave, weave, weave a circle of friendship
> People of faith, we can be strong.
> Love will bind us all together
> And will strengthen it with song.

(In the second verse 'love' in the third line is changed to 'hope', in the third verse, to 'peace', and in the fourth, to 'joy'.)

The ivy was placed round the central table.

Sharing

'Today we share bread and wine'

(Ann Peart in *The New Women Included*)

Bread and wine were passed round, with the words 'Food for the journey' and 'Cup of strength for our seeking'. To both of these the response was 'Maranatha – come Lord'.

Song

'Will you come and see the light?'
(Brian Wren)

2

New Year and Epiphany:
A Shared Meal

As has been suggested, many women's groups find it difficult to meet over the actual Christmas season, members preferring to celebrate with their own families. This liturgy, celebrated over a shared meal, combines the themes of beginning a New Year with a recollection of the gifts brought to the infant Jesus by the three wise men.

Setting

A large table set in a festive manner, with a small, decorated Christmas tree in the centre, and lit with many candles (low night-lights).

Elements

> A bowl of nuts and figs
> Gold foil wrapped chocolates
> Sachets of myrrh and frankincense
> Coloured papers and pens
> A simple meal of soup and bread, already prepared

Approximately a third of the candles were lit.

Introduction

Welcome to our liturgy which is a meal to celebrate the New Year and the feast of the Epiphany.

Participants, standing in a circle, said their names.

Prayer

All   This is the season of hope! Let the Spirit of Hope surround you.
Let your spirit rise to bless this new year.
O Great Spirit of Hope, blessed be your holy seasons.
Blessed be this season when we move to a new year.
Blessed be this magical time for new beginnings and fond farewells.
Blessed be this 'crack between the worlds' that we encounter at this season.
Blessed be this threshold place of transition between inside and outside.
Blessed be this transformation when spirits of hope and change gather.
Blessed be this passage from past securities to uncharted uncertainties.
Blessed be this shifting of emotions.
Blessed be this letting go of old hurts and pains.
Blessed be this reliable balancing act of nature.
Blessed be this rededication of values and meaning of life.
Oh Great Spirit of Hope, blessed be your holy season.

(Diann L. Neu)

Voice 1   This is a special meal at a special time with special people who have chosen or are able to be here on this first liturgy of the new year. So we shall eat together and look at the past, the present, the future, symbolized by the foods we shall eat and also by the gifts brought to the child Jesus, myrrh, frankincense and gold. These were all very, very rare and valuable at that time and we will learn a little about them by and by.

The Past
In our opening prayer we said 'Blessed be this letting go of old hurts and pains.' So what do we want to leave behind? What do we need forgiveness for? What have we learned and want to take forward? These are some of the questions we can share with our neighbour.

New Year and Epiphany: A Shared Meal

Participants split into pairs and shared their ideas in pairs for ten minutes.

Voice 1   We pass the nuts and figs and eat that which is good and to be taken forward. We throw shells and stalks into the bowl as a sign of truly letting go of old hurts and pains.

The figs and nuts were passed round and eaten.

Voice 2   Myrrh was one of the gifts brought to the new child Jesus. It is one of the very precious gifts of the past.

The myrrh was hung on the tree.
Every third person, taking their plate and glass with them, moved on to find different neighbours.
Half the remaining candles were lit.

Voice 2   Let us all together say this Jubilee prayer.

All   God of all ages, maker of time, mark of the alpha and point to the omega, Creator, Sustainer of everything living, touching us all who hold a hope with a vision that breaks through boundaries to grasp the blurred horizon. You gave your promise. A blessing of joy to those who have lost their faith in you. Now time is poised with renewed expectation of Emmanuel, God with us. To know our time of proclaimed favour, we make again the pledge you ask: 'Share justly the good things I give you. Reconcile with peace the rule of abuse. Give courage to those who voice the words of lives that have been silenced.'

Send us to carry your 'Good News' to those burdened with debt. Transfer their chains into clasps of love, of prayer, concern and then action.

Aware of your Spirit always among us, we sustain your purpose with passion. Increase our endeavour to do what you ask, that 'where there are wrongs, they be righted'. Now is the time. It will be achieved in acting justly, in loving tenderly and in walking humbly with you, our God.

(Lala Winkley, based on Matthew 11:2–5; Luke 4:17–19; Micah 6:8)

Voice 2   **The Present**
Now time is poised with renewed expectation of Emmanuel, God with us.
Now is the time for us to walk closely with you, our God.
Is God with you? Are you walking with God?
How? Perhaps another sentence speaks to you.
Take a new neighbour for these new questions.

The questions were discussed in pairs for about ten minutes.

Voice 2   We break bread and eat soup as the food for the present.

The rest of the meal was eaten.

Voice 3   Frankincense was another gift brought by the wise men to the infant Jesus. It is our symbol for the present.

The frankincense was hung on the tree.
Again every third person moved.
The rest of the candles were lit.

All   **This is the season of hope. Let the Spirit of Hope surround you. Let our spirit rise to bless this new year, this new year.**

Voice 1   What are your fears? What are your hopes for this new year?

Further discussion in pairs for about ten minutes.

Voice 1   We have food for the future. What else but gold!

The gold chocolates were passed round, and each person shared a hope.

Voice 2   At this time it is good to give and receive gifts. So we ask each of you to write an attribute that you would like to gift to another. We will put them all in the bowl face down and then everyone will receive from the 'lucky dip'.

New Year and Epiphany: A Shared Meal

The gifts were written down and shared.

Let us give each other a Kiss of Peace, for new beginnings, new hope!

3

Epiphany

This liturgy, like the previous one, celebrates the gifts of the wise men to the infant Jesus, but is not in the context of a meal. The original setting was associated with an Anglican church, and its theme was intended to express the combination of joy that women's ordination had been permitted in some denominations and hurt that it is still prohibited in others.

Elements

> Strips of white crêpe paper
> Candles
> Symbolic gifts – a Bible, a candle, oil

Introduction

As people gathered, white strips of paper were given to those belonging to churches that ordain women.

Song (Taizé)

'Veni Sancte Spiritus'

During the hymn, all linked hands and danced in a chain. An ordained woman, with lighted candle, invited those from churches that ordain women to have their candles lit.

Epiphany

Readings

'The Anointing' by Edwina Gateley
(from *Psalms of a Laywoman*)

Read by women whose churches deny ordination to women, gathering around the lighted candles of the others.

Isaiah 60 (Promise of the new Jerusalem)

During the second reading, the women whose candles were alight lit the candles of those whose churches still deny women's ordination.

All **Arise, shine out, for your light has come.**

Song and Prayers

The refrain 'Veni Sancte Spiritus' (Taizé) *was sung to accompany the petitions voiced by individual participants.*

Song

'We sing a love that sets all people free'

Enactment

As the individual gifts were brought forward these words were said:

'Three wise women' brought gifts to the table:
'Martha' brought the Bible, 'gold of wisdom';
'Mary Magdalene' brought a candle, as 'teller of the good news';
'The women who anointed Jesus' brought oil, 'the oil of priesthood'.

All placed candles near the gifts, going out into darkness, singing 'We shall overcome'.

4

Annunciation:
Women's World Day of Prayer

The Women's World Day of Prayer takes place annually on the Friday falling nearest to 8 March. This liturgy was performed near the Epstein statue of the Virgin and Child in Cavendish Square, London, but would be appropriate to any other location commemorating Mary or other valiant women; alternatively it could take place indoors, focusing on a central statue or picture.

Introduction

Gathering in a circle, each person said one line of a prayer; since it was the year of Jubilee, the Jubilee prayer (see page 63) was used, but other prayers or psalms could be substituted.

Calling

All said together: 'Rejoice!' One person in the circle said her own name, and everyone else repeated it and added, 'You are a special person. God loves you dearly.' This was repeated until everyone had been named.

Reading

Luke 1:26–38 (The Annunciation)

Song

'Holy Mary by God's decree' (first verse)

(An adaptation of 'Holy Virgin by God's decree', to be found in a number of hymnals, such as *Hymns Old and New*)

Sharing (in pairs or in the whole group if small)

When have you felt called and willing to act, saying yes to what you feel God is asking of you?

Song

'Holy Mary by God's decree' (second verse: 'With your faith and courageous reply . . .')

Prayers (said antiphonally)

A   Bless us, loving God, as we gather here for this liturgical action. Recognizing how you need our co-operation to realize your hopes for the world, on this designated day of prayer for women, we call for

All   **Reconciliation, justice and respect for all women.**

B   Faced with a global culture of women as inferior and the frequent pain of exclusion and abuse, we pray for renewed courage and persistence to continue our struggle, holding on to our hope for a just and wholesome world, so we sound the jubilee call for

All   **Reconciliation, justice and respect for all women.** (*Said*)
All   **Reconciliation, justice and respect for all, by all, within all.** (*Sung*)

A   This day has been chosen by our Church to ask forgiveness of women for the many times, over the two millennia of Christianity, that it has not treated women with dignity. Sound the call for

All   **Reconciliation, justice and respect by all, for all, within all.** (*Sung*)

B   We pause now to pray for women who today are damaged and suffering due to poor judgment and inappropriate pastoral treatment by the church authorities.

Recognizing this day as the one of world-wide prayer acknow-ledges the spectrum of discriminations and injustices forced on women, we pray that women's gifts, not their gender, be the criterion for ordination to the priesthood and episcopacy in Christian churches and in ministries of leadership in other religions. Let us sound the call for

All   **Reconciliation, justice and respect by all, for all, within all.** (*Sung*)

A   Our institution insists that exclusion from priesthood, due to gender, is part of revealed doctrine. All doctrines and laws must originate in scripture. Nowhere in scripture does it say that women cannot be priests. On the contrary, Mary was called and she said 'Yes'. Let us sound the call for

All   **Reconciliation, justice and respect by all, for all, within all.** (*Sung*)

B   Women are said to be unacceptable and unfit for priesthood; they are unable to image God in Christ. We are women because of a divine choice by our creator; we are created equally in God's image as all humanity. To prevent women being priests because as women we are told, we cannot image God, is a blasphemy. Let us sound the call for

All   **Reconciliation, justice and respect by all, for all, within all.** (*Sung*)

Collect

All   **Gathering the great contribution women have made to the Church through all its time, we give thanks, remembering all who have made and who are making the positive response of saying, 'Yes' to whatever you ask of them.**

Women of the past and present who gave inspiration were named.

In our prayer we pray for a metanoia, a conversion, to permeate right through our church, healing it of the evil sickness of 'institutionalized sexism'. We make this our silent pledge,
[*Each person held her right palm up in front.*]
in acceptance
[*Each person placed her left hand palm down on her neighbour's up-turned right palm.*]
and affirmation of each person here.

70

Silence

Song

'Holy Mary by God's decree' (third verse: 'Now in God's remnant Church of today')

Reading

In their 'appeal for unity', the Cricklade Statement of September 1995, Roman Catholic bishops of England and Wales stated how they had thought about the many ways in which communion within the church is fractured and frail. They say they know many people feel hurt and angry and are excluded. They recognize there are many ways in which the lives of people are bleeding . . . They say the church must become more conscious of the need for repentance. Of themselves, they find they sometimes exclude people whom Christ would welcome and therefore need to become a repentant, compassionate, reconciling Church, valuing the diversity which brings riches to our communion, fashioning new inclusive relationships as an example to the world of God's love.

Concluding Song – at choice

5

Annunciation

This feast commemorates Mary's agreement to become the mother of Christ, by which means he became incarnate to the world, and it has been argued that she thus became the first Christian priest. It therefore seemed particularly appropriate that this liturgy took place outside a cathedral church inevitably associated with clerical male power in the Roman Catholic Church, in this case, Westminster Cathedral. At one point, this setting became an integral part of the liturgy. It could, however, be adapted to other types of setting which symbolize male power, perhaps most easily by having a central picture of a cathedral if the liturgy were carried out indoors.

Elements

> Pictures of women
> Flowers
> A globe
> Oil
> Purple cloths

Introduction

Today on the Feast of the Annunciation, we come to celebrate and be in union with women and men world-wide, as we join in prayer for women's ordination all round the globe. Let us remember in silence all the women on all the continents, especially those of the third world and the poor of our world.

Annunciation

The names of the continents were placed around the globe.

Let us now be reminded of all the organizations round the world who work for women's ordination in the Roman Catholic Church.

Song

'Be still as we pray (3 times)
on our special day'

Reading

Luke 1:26–28 (The Annunciation)

Song

'Gospel-telling women, understanding women, we remember' (3 times)

Reading

Passages from Tissa Balasuriya, *Mary and Human Liberation*

Sharing

Let us share with each other our thoughts about Mary, and about third world women we know.

Flowers and pictures of women were placed around the globe.

Prayer (A Modern Magnificat)

All   My soul weeps, and my spirit lies battered within me
For the world belongs to the heartless imagination of the wealthy
And greed for profit and fear of war rule the earth;
The powerless go unheard and the hungry are not fed.
The poor and the weak are oppressed
And evil things are done in the name of this generation.
Arrogant men and submissive women

Squander the inheritance of our faith,
And seeds of hope are left to die in the dust.
Who will save our children for the promise of your mercy?
You who have looked with favour on your lowly servant Mary
will redeem your people in every generation.

Song

'Mary, woman of power,
Mary, woman of wisdom,
We have named you' (3 times)

The Blessing and Anointing with Oil

Voice 1 An act of anointing the head with oil is an ancient rite, signifying selection for some special role.

Voice 2 Let us now anoint each other on the forehead, showing the same courage and wisdom as that of Mary and all other courageous and wise women and men who have suffered for the truth, down the centuries and today.

Voice 3 Let us now anoint each other on the forehead, giving and sharing with each other the same courage and wisdom among ourselves.

Prayer for the Cathedral

Song (on the way to the cathedral walls)

'Be still and be strengthened (3 times)
As we pray by these walls'

Participants walked slowly and silently towards the cathedral holding purple cloths or wearing them like stoles.

They circled the cathedral and prayed in silence for seven minutes, one minute for each of the seven sacraments in the Catholic tradition (Baptism, Confirmation, Holy Communion, Penance, Matrimony, Holy Order, Last Anointing). They then returned to the initial point, singing quietly.

Song

'Renewed with God's silence (3 times)
And strengthened in faith'

Prayer for Women's Ordination

(Read by five people standing facing out from the globe)

Moved by a compulsion of the Holy Spirit,
we cannot remain ignorant of this injustice in our midst.

We long for all humanity to be acknowledged as equal,
particularly among our community of the Church,
so we pray, grieving for the lost gifts of so many women.

We ask you, God of all peoples,
to bring insight and humility to all those in positions of dominance,
and an understanding that the ascended Lord called us all to act,
doing Christ's work here and now.

We ask this of you,
God our Creator,
Jesus our Redeemer,
Spirit our Sustainer.

Song at the Sign of Peace

'Embrace peace and justice (3 times)
And love as Christ loved'

6

Maundy Thursday: The Oils of Suffering
Remembering the woman who anointed Jesus with chrism, and women's ordination

This liturgy was performed outside a cathedral building, inside which the priests of the diocese were carrying out the celebration of the 'chrism' mass, during which the oils to be used in the sacraments were blessed. References are therefore made to the priests of the diocese coming out after the celebration. If this liturgy were performed inside, a picture representing exclusive male involvement in such ceremonies could be substituted.

Elements

> Candles
> Oils
> Stories of women of the past
> Purple scarves
> Sandwich boards, naming the women whose stories will be told

Song

'God, our Creator, Christ our Anointer, Spirit our Healer'
(in unison, then as a three-part round)

Welcome

We are gathered here today at the appointed time of the diocesan Mass of Chrism. The chrism mass being celebrated now inside this cathedral is a service of the renewal of their priestly vows by the men accepted as priests in this diocese, and the blessings of the chrism oils to be used by the priests in their parish baptisms.

Our celebration out here is a ceremony of the anointing of all the Priestly People of God. We are calling on women and men to share with us the responsibility to helping our church, our society, our world, to see that it must rid itself of clinging to unjust ways.

As Pope John Paul II has said that the models of male domination must be rejected in every aspect of the life of our society, and that we are today acknowledging and affirming the true genius of women who suffer daily the evil of discrimination, violence and exploitation, yet constantly search and work for a gospel of life.

We take our theme from the woman who anointed Jesus.

The Past

Song

'Gospel-telling woman, understanding woman, we remember'
(first in unison then as a three-part round)

Reading

Mark 14:1–9 (A woman anoints Jesus)
In memory of her – a loving anonymous woman.

Song

'Gospel-telling women, understanding women, we remember'
(in unison, then as a three-part round)

Prayer

All Let us now praise wonderful and strong women like our fore-mothers who lived before us, through whom God's glory has been shown in each successive generation.

77

Song

'Women of power, women of struggle, we remember'
(three-part round, sung once)

Prayer

All   Some women have left a name to be remembered. But others are lost to memory. The nameless women of each age, as though they had never been, are now left forgotten in history.

Song

'Forgotten women, women who built our world, we remember'
(three-part round, sung once)

Prayer

All   Today their glory we extol. We sing of these women, our mothers unnamed, declaring their wisdom with pride and joy.

Song

'Women of wisdom, women of joy, we extol you'
(three-part round, sung once)

Women's Stories

A brief reference was made to some of the women whose lives still inspire us, for instance: Hilda, Abbess of Whitby, who traditionally is thought to have encouraged the poet Caedmon; Julian of Norwich, who recognized the motherhood of God; Mary Ward, who travelled boldly through a hostile country, bringing the good news of God.

While the stories were being told, slowly each woman in turn processed in silence from the edge to the centre of the circle and back, so that the words on their sandwich boards could be read by everybody.

After everyone had thus made their silent statement

All   We are on a journey to bring justice and liberation to all the women of the world. We have vision that the struggles of our foremothers will not be in vain.

We dream dreams for our daughters and granddaughters,
that they may stand upright and strong in their lives and work,
taking on the tasks required of them.

Song

'God our Creator, Christ our Anointer, Spirit our Healer'
(three-part round sung once, then hummed)

The Present

Voice 1   An act anointing the head with oil is an ancient rite, signifying selection for some special role or task.

Ritual of Blessing the Oil

Voice 2   For our chrism oil we use plant oil, blended with sweet lavender and rosemary for remembrance. Let us stretch out our hand to bless this oil, wordless as the woman whose model we follow today.

Those present stretched out their hands in blessing over the oils in the centre of the circle, holding hands in silence.

Voice 3   Let us now anoint each other on the forehead showing the same caring courage as the nameless gospel woman who refused to remain an onlooker. We want to strengthen each other in our endeavours, respecting the special calling to all to be a priestly people seeking justice.

The three speakers brought oils to three points of the circle; each person anointed the forehead of the person to her left and if she wished spoke words of her choice. The oil was passed on round the circle to the left, anointing the next person and so on. After being anointed, each person used the purple cloth to seal in the strengthening oils by covering their brows.

Prayer for the Cathedral

All   We pray for the cathedral building, cleansing it with our blessed oil on our sealing purple cloths. The cathedral church and the altar it houses are said to represent the body of Christ. We see it now distorted into a place of power, housing an unjust system of domination by patriarchy. We sing of that space, which is not a woman's space.

While singing the following, participants slowly moved to encircle the cathedral building, shrouding the stone walls with the purple cloths which had been used to cover their foreheads, praying for it as the stones were touched. Singing continued until all had walked around the cathedral building. Singing gradually became softer.

Song

'Be still and be strengthened (3 times)
To pray for that space'

Silence for seven minutes, followed by gentle singing.

Song

'Renewed with God's silence (3 times)
Go into the world' (repeated)

Participants moved away from the cathedral building to form a circle on the pavement again.

Song

'Embrace peace and justice (3 times)
To love and be loved'

Prayer

All   Moved by a compulsion of the Holy Spirit,
       we cannot remain ignorant of this injustice in our midst.

We long for all humanity to be acknowledged as equal,
particularly among your community of the Church,
so we pray, grieving for the lost gifts of so many women.

We ask you, God of all peoples,
to bring insight and humility to all those in positions of dominance,
and an understanding that the ascended Lord has called us all to act,
doing Christ's work here and now.

We ask this of you,
God our Creator,
Jesus our Redeemer,
Spirit our Sustainer.

The Future

Voice 1   Being anointed holds a responsibility. In a spirit of rejuvenation and renewal, we work to inform others. Our action is to ask thought-provoking questions about the place of women in the Church to our parish priest or any one who we feel still remains in ignorance and prejudice.

Blessing

Voice 1   Before we go forth to take our message of conversion, let us bless each other.

People placed their right hands on their neighbours' left shoulders.

Song

'Come Spirit circle us, fill us with hope, keep love alive' (3 times)

Everyone moved to their right, stood still, looked at the person being blessed, and said:

Prayer

All Come, Creator of us all, bless us as we bless each other, seeing in each one of us, the image of God. No longer can we be onlookers. Let us see our action as prophetic and be daring in our love of God, which may lead us to places we would rather not go.

The song 'Come Spirit circle us' was repeated while moving, then people stood still and said:

All Come, Christ, who bade us weep, make all our tears and silenced voices a bridge to our understanding of the reality of politics, the dimensions of ethics, the perspectives on our environment, and may our stories of daily experiences never more be scorned.

The song 'Come Spirit circle us' was repeated again while moving, then people stood still and said:

All Come, Holy Spirit, awakening in us dangerous dreams of a new tomorrow where to live is to change, for we are carriers of a new vision that spirals constantly in a deeper understanding of the Trinity's dream for us to be creative, loving and free-spirited. We are called to be.

Song

'Women of the gospel, courageous women, women of wisdom'

All We are committed to conversion, to grow into a community of disciples, called to live simply, to love tenderly, to act justly.

Song

'Come Spirit circle us, fill us with hope, keep love alive'
(in unison, then as a three-part round)

Kiss of Peace

Voice 1 Let us give each other a kiss of peace.

Maundy Thursday: The Oils of Suffering

Song

(This was sung while priests were coming out from the Mass of Chrism in the cathedral.)

Let us break bread together and be one.
Let us break bread together in God's Name,
When we break bread together
Your body is broken too.
We share your mercy and love.

7

Passover

This Seder, a commemoration of the 'passing over of the Lord' is a Jewish ritual which has increasingly been adapted by Christians for use on Maundy Thursday, recalling the Last Supper of Jesus with his disciples. On this occasion, the ritual began in darkness, in a garden, a setting that provided the opportunity to make a fire, an essential part of this liturgy. Participants then went in to a dining room, in which they would eat the passover meal. The four cups of wine and the asking of questions are integral to the ritual; other elements, notably the woolly lamb, are innovative.

Elements

> Fire
> A woolly lamb
> Food, including matzos (unleavened bread), green leaves (salad or spinach) and wine
> Symbols of slavery (at participants' choice)
> Salt water
> Candles
> A gong

Introduction

God calls us from slavery to freedom. When we respond to this call, we must leave behind our chains, whatever enslaves us, and follow in haste, unencumbered by the weight of past oppression.

The fire was lit.

Blessing

All Blessed are you, Lord our God, Sovereign of the Universe. You sanctify us by your commandments, and teach us to kindle the festival fire. We light a fire, to burn the leaven of the old life. We will be slaves no longer. One by one, we throw into the fire our symbols of slavery.

The symbols of slavery were burnt up in the flames of the new fire. Participants gathered in the dining room and the candles were lit.

All May the festival lights we now kindle inspire us to use our power to heal and not to harm, to help and not to hinder, to bless and not to curse, to serve you, God of freedom.

A woolly lamb was the sign of authority at this feast. The person holding the lamb for the time being was termed the 'Voice' and passed the lamb on when she felt she wanted to pass on the role of Voice.

The first cup of wine, the cup of memory, was poured but not drunk.

Voice God calls each of us to freedom. As we drink the first cup of wine, we recall the promise.

All I am the One Who Is and I will free you from the burdens of slavery. We praise you, O God, Creator of the Universe, who makes the fruit of the vine.

All drunk the first cup of wine.

Voice A reading from the Song of Songs:
Arise my beloved, my fair one, and come away. For see, the winter is past. Flowers appear on the earth. The time of singing is here. The song of the dove is heard in our land. Let us go down to the vineyards to see if the vines have budded. There I will give you my love.

All Green leaves speak to us of spring, of the rebirth of hope, and of the wonder of creation.

Song

A song appropriate to the season was sung.

Voice We dip the green leaves in salt water to remind ourselves of the bitter tears of the oppressed, the slaves, of people without hope.

The green leaves were dipped in the salt water, but not eaten yet.

A poem from a women's writing project was read.

All We praise you, O God, giver of life, of hope, of laughter, maker of the fruits of the earth.

The green leaves dipped in salt water were eaten. A plate of matzos was uncovered, and one matzo drawn from the middle and broken.

Voice Among people everywhere, sharing bread forms a bond of friendship. Later, we will hunt for the *afikoman*, that is, this matzo which is for all, and share it.

The matzo – the afikoman *– was taken away to be hidden.*

Voice While it is being hidden, let us remember together all who are in need, the unjustly imprisoned, the homeless, those who are in despair.

The plate of matzos was held up.

All This is the bread of poverty, the poor bread, which our mothers baked in the land of Egypt.
Let all who are hungry come and eat. Let all who are in want share the hope of Passover. Now we are here: Next year may we be in Jerusalem. Now we are still enslaved: Next year may all be free.

The matzos were broken and distributed.

All   We praise you, O God, for the bread you bring forth from the earth.

The matzos were eaten.

The Four Questions

Each question is asked by the youngest person present.

The First Question: Why is this night different from all other nights?

Voice   Let us remember and never forget: how God called us out of Egypt, and empowered us to break the bonds of slavery.

The Second Question: Why do we eat matzos tonight, instead of ordinary bread?

Voice   Let us remember and never forget: when God called us out of Egypt, we went in haste. There was no time to wait for dough to rise. So we eat matzos, recalling the hard, flat bread that sustained us as we fled into the desert.

The Third Question: Why do we eat bitter herbs tonight?

Voice   Let us remember and never forget the bitterness of slavery, and remember that even today many of our sisters and brothers are enslaved: by poverty, by ignorance, by anger, by greed, by wealth, by success.

The Fourth Question: Why do we come together tonight to celebrate this feast?

Voice   Let me remember and never forget: my mother was a wandering Aramean, and with her husband and sons she went down into Egypt, fleeing from famine, and settled there. In Egypt she bore children, sons and daughters, and her sons were drowned at birth, but her daughters were spared to bear children in their turn, slaves for the Egyptians. And the slaves were ill-treated, beaten and abused.

All   Then we called to the God of our mothers, of Sarah, Hagar, Rebecca, of Rachel, Leah and Tamar, and God heard our voice and saw our toil and oppression and . . .

Voice   A Hebrew slave bore a son in Egypt. She was determined that he should live, and helped by her daughter and midwife, concealed the baby until he was weaned. Then she placed him in a basket in the reeds by the Nile where Pharaoh's daughter came to bathe, and so the child was taken from the river into the household of the princess, and she loved him as her own son.

Voice   As a young man, in anger he killed an overseer who was beating a slave, one of his own people. He fled from Egypt, and came to Horeb, and there God called to him out of a bush that burned brighter than the sun, but did not burn away.

All   I am the God of your people, the God of Abraham and Sarah, the God of Rebecca and Isaac, the God of Rachel, of Jacob, of Leah. I have seen the misery of my people in Egypt, I have heard their outcry, I have seen the brutality of their oppressors. I have come to rescue them from slavery, to lead them out of bondage. I will send you to Pharaoh, and you shall bring my people out of Egypt.

Song

'Go down Moses', with refrain, 'Let my people go'

All   God heard our weeping and remembered the promise and God knew.

Voice   What did God know?

All   When the Israelites had grown accustomed to their tasks, when the Hebrews began to labour without complaint, then God knew it was time that they be liberated.

Voice   For the worst slavery of Egypt is when we learn to endure it! And God knew . . .

All   As long as there was no prospect of freedom, God knew the Israelites would not awaken to the bitterness of bondage. First

Moses had to teach the taste of freedom's hope, and only then did servitude taste bitter.

Voice So though bitter slavery is first, and then comes liberation, the Seder teaches us to taste the matzo of freedom first. And God knew . . .

All If our freedom had been given us by Pharaoh, we would have been indebted to him, still subservient, within ourselves dependent, slavish still at heart. We had to free ourselves!

Voice And because we freed ourselves, ever after, even when demeaned by others and suffering privation, within ourselves we always wanted to be free!

All The God-inspired know that people must aspire to the service of the Highest in order to be free.

Voice Others can gain control of you so long as you possess a will distinct from God's.

All And God knew.

Wine glasses were filled again.

Voice Moses went to Pharaoh, and demanded that he set the Hebrews free. But Pharaoh refused. And God said, I will go through the land of Egypt, and I will see justice done, I, the Eternal.

All And the Holy One, blessed be he, brought us out of Egypt by a mighty hand, by an outstretched arm and mighty power, and by signs and portents.

All raised their cups: but did not drink.

Voice The sword comes into the world because of justice delayed and justice denied. To recall the strife and distress that follows oppression, we pour ten drops of wine for the plagues upon Egypt. Each drop of wine is hope and prayer that we may cast out the plagues that threaten us all, wherever they are found, beginning in our own hearts.

A gong was used to mark each plague.

Voice	Blood	*All*	**War**
	Frogs		**Hate**
	Lice		**Pollution**
	Wild beasts		**Injustice**
	Blight		**Violence**
	Boils		**Indifference**
	Hail		**Oppression**
	Locusts		**Corruption**
	Darkness		**Ignorance**
	Slaying of the first-born		**Despair**

The wine cups were set down again on the table, the wine untasted.

Silence

Voice Let us reflect on the gifts God gives to us.
All   **For that alone we would have been grateful.**

Voice Had he brought us out of Egypt and not fed us in the desert:
All   **For that alone we would have been grateful.**

Voice Had he fed us with the manna, and not then ordained the Sabbath:
All   **For that alone we would have been grateful.**

Voice Had he then ordained the Sabbath, and not brought us to Mount Sinai:
All   **For that alone we would have been grateful.**

Voice Had he brought us to Mount Sinai, and not given us the Torah:
All   **For that alone we would have been grateful.**

Voice Had he given us the Torah, and not led us into Israel:
All   **For that alone we would have been grateful.**

Voice Had he led us into Israel, and not given us the prophets:
All   **For that alone we would have been grateful.**

Voice Let us now raise the second cup of wine, the cup of redemption. We remember with gratitude our liberation from Egypt, we rejoice in the fruits of our struggle for freedom. We look with hope to the future.

All We praise you Lord our God, Sovereign of the universe, who creates the fruit of the vine.

The cup of redemption was drunk. The Seder meal was then eaten. Between the main course and pudding, everyone was invited to hunt for the afikoman, *with a prize for the person finding it.*

The afikoman *was divided and eaten with the coffee, but nothing was eaten after it, making it the last food tasted.*

Song

Psalm 126: 'When the Lord delivered Zion from bondage'

Voice Let us say grace together.

All The name of the Eternal be blessed now and forever.
We give thanks to you, God.
We give thanks as we invoke your name, as we recount your marvels.

Voice We thank you for your mercy and compassion.

All May we always share what we have with those in need.

Voice We thank you for liberation from slavery.

All May we always hunger and thirst for justice.
All Merciful, make us worthy of the Messianic promise of the world that is yet to be.

Voice May the One who blessed our mothers and fathers bless this house, and everyone gathered at this table, and all those we love. God will give strength to the people.

All God will bless all people with peace.

The wine cups were filled for the third time: the cup of deliverance.

All We praise you, Lord our God, life of the universe, who creates the fruit of the vine.

Voice Elijah the prophet from the village of Tishbe in Gilead challenged the injustice of the king. He healed the sick, he helped the weak, he cared for the widowed. He left this earth, carried to skies in a whirlwind and a chariot of fire. The injustice of the world still brings to mind Elijah, who in defence of justice challenged the powerful. Jewish legend has it that from time to time Elijah returns to the earth, to befriend the friendless, to seek shelter with the humble, to remind God's people of their coming freedom. We pour this wine for Elijah, to welcome the prophet to our feast.

All **May the All Merciful send us Elijah the prophet to comfort us with good news of our salvation.**

Voice For every undecided question of pain and sorrow, of unrewarded worth and unrequited evil, Elijah, so it is said, will someday provide the answer.

All **There are links between heaven and earth which promise an answer to our questions.**

Voice Elijah opens for us the door to the realm of mystery and wonder. Let us now open the door for Elijah.

The youngest person present was sent to open a door to the outside. As the door was opened, all said:

Come Elijah, we have waited long, we have lived with many questions. We are full of wonder.

Voice From past and future, Elijah enters, and tastes with us the wine of the promise:

All **I will bring you into the land – I, the Lord.**

Voice We lift the cup of deliverance, and call upon the name of God.

All **We will praise God forever.**

The cup of deliverance was drunk.

Song

Psalm 136: 'Great is God's Love, Love without End'

(Derived from the Grail version, numbered as Psalm 135, 'Great is his love, love without end')

Voice   God is my strength and my song, and God has become my salvation.

All   **We will praise our God forever!**

Voice   Let us sing in celebration of our freedom.

Song

On this occasion, 'Green grow the rushes' was sung; other celebratory songs could be chosen.

A single cup of wine was passed, and held up.

Voice   It is still dark as we pour this cup, but light dawns over Zion. We raise this cup, the cup of freedom, for the day when we will tell of the liberation of all. We set aside this cup as a sign of hope of our redemption.

All   **We praise you, Lord our God, Sovereign of existence, who has sanctified us with your commandment, and commanded us to renew the hope of redemption.**

The cup was set down.

Voice   As the Seder draws to an end, once again we fill our cups of wine. Salvation is not yet complete.

The cups of wine were filled for the fourth time: the cup of acceptance.

Voice   The cup of acceptance recalls us to the tasks that still await us as people called to the service of God.

All   **We praise you, Lord our God, Sovereign of the universe, with whom we journey together in hope.**

All drank the fourth cup: the cup of acceptance.

Voice   The Seder is now over. The rites have been observed, the story told, the mysteries shared.

Next year may we celebrate again together, in joy, in freedom, in peace.

All   Peace! For us, for everyone!
For all peoples, this is our hope.
Next year, in Jerusalem!
Next year, may all be free!

Song (tune: Finlandia)

'Go forth in faith'

8

Easter

This liturgy took place in a garden and a room adjacent to it. It could be performed inside if the garden was in some way symbolized – by pictures, plants, etc. An Easter garden, as frequently constructed in churches, would be a good way of providing a symbol of both death and resurrection.

Elements

> Eggs
> Candles
> Material for lighting a fire

Introduction: Waiting in Gethsemane

Readings

Sung response after each reading: 'Stay here and watch with me' (Taizé)

'I said to my soul, be still'
(from 'East Coker', the second of T. S. Eliot's *Four Quartets*)

'The work of winter starts fermenting'
(from *The Spirit of Place* in *The Fact of a Doorframe* by Adrienne Rich)

It would appear that those today who wait upon the Lord should draw inspiration and courage from the gospel traditions of religious disobedience to oppressive conventions . . . and radical protest, in particular on behalf of those who are marginalised and exploited. This applies of course to all those who are abused and exploited in today's world. It also applies to those who are discriminated against or excluded in

today's church, whether from the ecclesiastical community as a whole or from the assemblies for worship and its ministerial structures.
(Andree Heaton, *The Candles are Still Burning*)

I have always remained at this exact point, on the threshold of the church, without moving . . . only now my heart has been transported, forever I hope, into the Blessed sacrament.
(Simone Weil, *Waiting on God*)

By our activity of loving we destine ourselves in the end to waiting – to placing in the hands of another the outcome of our own endeavour and to exposing ourselves to receiving from those hands the triumph or tragedy of our own endeavour . . . where love is, action is destined to pass into passion, working into waiting. The intimate connection between loving and waiting is expressed in familiar and popular ways in the representation of the lover as waiting figure.
(W. H. Vanstone, *The Stature of Waiting*)

Prayers and Reflections

The emphasis was on people and groups who are waiting.

Participants were then asked to go into the garden for the lighting of the Easter fire, from which their own candles could be lit.

Reading

John 20:11–18 (The Easter Gospel, of Mary Magdalene waiting in the garden)

Participants were invited to take an egg and offer a word of 'egging on' or encouragement, or 'cracking open' in envisaging new beginnings to each other and the earth.

Blessing

Song

'Now the green blade riseth'
(*Twentieth-Century Folk Hymnal*)

9

Pentecost

The symbolism in this liturgy is intended to reflect various aspects of the Holy Spirit, coming with power at this season of the Church's year.

Elements

> A branch and some blossoming twigs
> Shells
> A loaf of bread

Introduction

Song

'Spirit of Fire'

(All the songs in this liturgy are by June Boyce-Tillman, from her *In Praise of All Encircling Love*, Vol. 1.)

Introduction to the Readings

There are various strands that come together in our understanding of the Holy Spirit and which led to the development of the concept of the Trinity, which evolved in post-biblical times.

Readings

Breath

One aspect of the Spirit is *Ruah* (Hebrew) or breath – something dynamically in movement and impossible to constrain. According to

Elizabeth Johnson (in the book *She Who Is*): 'Divine Spirit is not understood to be independently personal, as its symbolization in wind, fire, light and water makes clear, but is the creative and freeing power of God let loose in the world. More than most terms for God's dynamism it evokes a universal perspective and signifies divine activity in its widest reaches.'

Wisdom

Another strand is that of Wisdom, or Sophia. In the Hebrew scriptures this is one way of understanding the action of God, and is often portrayed as a personified (and female) figure. Sophia represents both the transcendent and the active presence of God among human beings: 'From everlasting I was firmly set, from the beginning, before earth came into being' (Proverbs 8:23). She is a life giver, a preacher of reproach, punishment and promise, and her ways are those of insight, life and peace. She is associated with the Torah and pitches her tent among the people.

Song

'Hymn to Wisdom'

Readings

Energizer and Connector

Mary Grey in *Wisdom of Fools* emphasizes the Spirit as primarily an energizer who is continually 'renewing the face of the earth' (Psalm 104:30).

The theology of the spirit has been very underdeveloped until recent times. Today liberation and feminist theologies are leading to its emergence as the energy of connectedness, one that is experienced as the breath of life, the vitality of the rhythms of creation, a force that leads to justice making and a relational power that binds us in community.

Older intuitions saw the Spirit as the 'Church' but this was identified with the institution, whereas today the Spirit is increasingly understood as 'the relational principle, searching for new manifestations of the gathered people of God.' In her chapter 'Revelation and Connected Knowing' (from the book quoted above), Mary Grey connects Sophia with a different way of knowing: one that is connected, does not separate the knower and the known, bodily feeling and detached logic, which is the hidden wisdom of the natural world, and acknowledges our mutual interdependence.

We need to transform the root metaphors by which our culture understands itself, our relationships and our politico-social structures, if we are to eradicate the roots of oppression in society and religion.

Nurturer and Birther

The question has been asked, is the spirit the female dimension of the spirit divine? Too much can be made of grammatical gender (*ruah* and other words associated with the spirit such as Sophia, wisdom, and *shekinah*, presence, being feminine). More meaningful is the female imagery associated with the activity of the spirit: the mother bird hovering or brooding over the waters to bring life, the birthing imagery in connection with the birth and baptism of Jesus, the rebirth/ new life brought to the believer by the Spirit through the waters of baptism.

Particularly the hovering, sheltering and protecting aspects of the Holy Spirit have been seen as female.

(All readings were taken from The Holy Spirit: Long-distance learning course module, British and Irish School of Feminist Theology, Ianthe Pratt.)

Song

'Urban Spirit'

Reading

The Holy Spirit is a Burning Spirit. It kindles the hearts of humankind.
Holy Spirit is life-giving-life, all movement.
Root of all being. Absolver of all faults.
Balm of all wounds.

Radiant life, worthy of all praise,
the Holy Spirit resurrects and awakens everything that is.
The Spirit is an unquenchable fire, bestows all excellence, sparks all worth,
awakes all goodness, ignites speech, enflames humankind.
Yet in this radiance is a restorative stillness.
It is the stillness that is similarly in the will to good. It spreads to all sides.
You are the mighty way in which everything that is in the heavens,
on the earth and under the earth,
is penetrated with connectedness,
is penetrated with relatedness.
You are the source of human understanding.
You bless with the breath of wisdom.
(from *Uhlein's Meditations with Hildegard of Bingen*)

Blossoming twigs were bound on to a branch, to symbolize the regenerative power of the spirit.

Prayer

'Exuberant Spirit of God'
(Jan Berry in *Bread of Tomorrow*)

Intercessions

Shells were laid in a spiral as each prayer was made.

Blessing of the Food

All We share this loaf today, as a sign that we are all one in the body of Christ.
Just as many grains come together into the one loaf, so we are all one in Christ Jesus.
Help us to reflect the life giving love of the Creator, Redeemer and Spirit in all our relationships and actions.

On passing the bread, each said to the person next to them, 'May this bread sustain you on your journey.'

Circle Dance and Song

'Come Spirit, circle us, keep love within, evil outside'

Harvest

The gathering in of harvest has often been a season for celebration in church, especially in rural communities. In this liturgy is it also symbolically linked with the seasons of our own lives.

Elements

Chairs
A red and orange cloth
A loaf of bread
A dish of wheat grain
Berries, leaves, fresh fruits of autumn
A bowl of earth

Setting

The chairs were set in a circle with the orange cloth on the floor in the centre. The loaf of bread and dish of wheat grain were placed on the cloth.

Voice 1 Love is not changed by death. The theme of our liturgy is Harvest. On the cloth are many signs of harvest and autumn. We will pass the dish of wheat grain and as you each hold it say your name.

The dish is passed round the circle.

Voice 1 Now is the time of harvest. We see all around us signs in the colours of autumn, in the abundance of berries, in the new fruits in the shops. In our society with freezers and sophisticated canning, there are no longer seasonal foods but this harvest/autumn is surely telling us something. I invite you to turn to your neighbour and consider the following questions:

What are your feelings about harvest and autumn?
What does it tell you about yourself and your life?

The questions were discussed in pairs for about ten minutes.

Voice 1   Now I invite you to take a fruit, berries, leaves – some piece that is a good symbol for you and appeals to you. Now place your chosen object on the cloth, and, if you wish, say something about the reflection you have just had with your neighbour.

Voice 2   John in chapter 12 verse 24 says, 'Unless a wheat grain falls on the ground and dies, it remains only a single grain; but if it dies it yields a rich harvest.' We will reflect on this idea.

Silence for five minutes

Voice 1   People who live on the land, as peoples in Africa and India and South America do, know how important it is not to eat all the crop. Some grain must be kept to be planted for the next year's crop. So take a wheat grain and plant it as a symbol of your own hopes for yourself. As you plant it, feel free to speak or not, you may want to say something about your reflection on John's verse.

Everyone planted a grain.

Voice 1   That was the seed corn. The harvest is here in this bread which we will bless and share.

The bread was held up and the blessing said in an antiphonal mode, the last two lines being said all together.

Blessing

'The Blessing of the Bread'
(Carter Heyward in *The New Women Included*)

The bread was passed round the circle, each breaking a piece and giving it to the next person saying: 'By the power of women, by the power of God you are blessed.'

Closing Prayer

All   The dying vegetation drops to the ground and forms the new fertile earth for the sowing of next year's crop. The grain is planted and breaks in the earth, sending down roots and sending up a shoot. That shoot bears a myriad of grains. For something to grow, something must die. May we, as bringers of life, know when to let go in order to have new life.

THEMES

11

Images of God

No single image is adequate for the infinity and variety of God. Too often, people have been forced into thinking of God in limited, often male terms, and both theology and action have been affected by this limitation. This liturgy is intended to help participants to acknowledge divine variety.

Elements

> Grapes
> Bread and wine
> Candles
> Pens
> Papers cut into leaf shapes
> A branch of a tree
> A large sheet of paper
> A small basket or other container

Introduction

Song

'Bring Many Names'
(Brian Wren in *Bring Many Names*)

Asking for Forgiveness

This was read round the group in turn, all responding as indicated.

Reader	O God, Creator, Redeemer and Sustainer, Pattern of mutual love, forgive us for failing to understand that being Church means loving well.
All	**Help us to create loving community.**
Reader	God of justice and integrity, forgive us for our offences against solidarity with other women, and for the times we have put down others.
All	**Help us to uphold each other.**
Reader	O God the disturber, forgive us for the times when we have sought security in the familiar rather than going out to seek new life in the wilderness.
All	**Help us to be joyful pilgrims trusting in your guidance.**
Reader	God, maker of both women and men in your own image, forgive us for colluding in sexist distortions.
All	**Help us to have confidence in ourselves.**
Reader	O Creator God, forgive us for not affirming the goodness of the bodies you have given us, and for forgetting the importance of Mary caressing Jesus' feet with her hair (John 12:1–8).
All	**Help us to accept ourselves in our God-given wholeness.**
Reader	O God, friend and lover, forgive us for our failing to understand our calling to friendship and honesty.
All	**Help us to be creative and healing in our relationships.**
Reader	O God, source of all insight, forgive us our shallow understanding of sacrament, when we fail to recognize the meal taken together, the joy or sorrow shared as a meeting with the divine.
All	**Help us to recognize where you are among us.** **O Spirit that empowers the powerless, give us the strength to forge communities of loving friends who seek to bring about the new life promised in the resurrection.**

Discussion (in pairs or threes)

Unhelpful names or images of God

Names for these unhelpful images were written on a large sheet of paper. When finished it was passed round the group so that everyone could help tear it up. The pieces were put in a basket.

Psalm (said antiphonally)

Virtually all the psalms make extensive use of imagery about God; examples are Psalm 18 or Psalm 27, but others could equally well be chosen.

Readings (read around the group)

All language about God is metaphorical. It has been claimed that it is a form of idolatry when we mistake the image for the reality. 'While we are immediately aware that the personal God is not really a rock or a mother eagle, it is easy enough to imagine God is really a king or a father'.

(Sandra Schneiders, *Women and the Word*)

Rosemary Radford Ruether (*Sexism and God Talk*) points out that Jesus' use of 'Abba' for his Father affirms a relationship based on love and trust that transforms the patriarchal concept of fatherhood into a more maternal and nurturing role. The early Jesus movement used the concept of God as Abba to liberate the community from dominant-subordinate relationships. Unfortunately this did not last and much of the language we now use reinforces patriarchal images.

God as covenant maker: 'This is the covenant I shall make with the House of Israel . . . Deep within them I shall plant my Law, writing it on their hearts. Then I shall be their God and they will be my people' (Jeremiah 31:33–4).

'I am the one who taught Israel to walk . . . I drew them to me with love and affection, I picked them up and held them to my cheek, I knelt down to them and fed them' (Hosea 11). When the people of Israel claimed the Lord had abandoned them the answer was, 'Can a woman forget her own body and love not the child she bore' (Isaiah 49:15). The key biblical concept of compassion – pity, mercy, tender loving-kindness – comes from a root word meaning womb.

'God is light, and there is no darkness in God at all' (1 John 1:5). 'We know we have come to know God, if we keep the commandments' (1 John 2:3). 'Whoever fails to love does not know God, because God is love' (1 John 4:8).

'Anyone who has seen me has seen the Father . . . I am in the Father and the Father is in me' (John 19:9–10).

Discussion (in pairs or threes)

What images of God have we personally found the most relevant in our spiritual journey?

Haikus (poems with 5–7–5 syllables) were then composed, individually or collectively, on helpful images of God. These were written on leaf-shaped papers and put on the 'tree' (the twigs or branch). The following haiku uses the ocean as an image of God:

> Life maker, storm surge, wave
> Chaos in creative order
> First mystery, last resource.
> (Patricia Stoat)

Song

'The Bird of Heaven'
(Sydney Carter, *The Present Tense*)

Intercessions

Candles were lit as each individual said her prayer.

Sharing

All   We share together these grapes, reminding ourselves how we are branches and fruit of the one true vine: This metaphor gives us a vision of the Christian community as a community of inter-relationship, mutuality and indwelling.

The grapes were passed around.

All In wine the fruit of the vine is crushed and becomes one, uniting us in a cup strengthening us for the journey.

The cup of wine was passed, with the words, 'May the fruit of the vine energize you.'

The bread was blessed, all saying:

> We share this loaf today, as a sign that we are all one in the body of Christ. Just as many grains come together into the one loaf, so we are all one in Christ Jesus.
> Help us to reflect the life giving love of the Creator, Redeemer and Spirit in all our relationships and actions.

The bread was passed round, with the words: 'Bread for the journey.'

Song

'Mother God'
(*Reflecting Praise*)

or

'God the All-Holy' (tune: Morning has broken)

12

Seeing

We know that what and how each individual sees depends to a very large extent on all her previous experience of life and perceiving. This liturgy is intended to encourage participants to respect both their own and other people's modes of seeing.

Elements

Bread
Candles
Mirrors

Introduction

'For now we see in a mirror dimly, but then we will see face to face.'
(1 Corinthians 13:12)

This liturgy is about how we see things; different people see the same thing very differently.

Examples could be given at this point – for instance, different descriptions of the same street, or a painting.

We are going to explore how we see. To introduce ourselves we will pass a mirror and each person is invited to say her name and whatever else she wants to say about what she sees in the mirror.

Seeing

Prayer

All   Spirit of God, Giver of Life
       Moving between us and around, like wind or water or fire;
       Breathe into us your freshness that we may awake;
       Cleanse our vision that we may see more clearly;
       Kindle our senses that we may feel more sharply;
       And give us the courage to live
       As you would have us live.

Discussion

Participants were asked to spend a moment thinking about something that they consider beautiful, to concentrate on it, savour and enjoy it. Then in pairs or groups they were asked to discuss: 'What did I see?' 'Why was it beautiful?', 'Would the others in the group think it beautiful?' Back in the whole group, each person was asked to report in one sentence on what was 'seen'. They were then asked to reflect on how the way that we see reflects the way that we live.

Reading

Christ in us knows both the loneliness of the outsider and the crabbed lives of the insider. He experiences in us the full diversity of the human condition. The meeting of Christ in us with the Christ in others will mean that we shall be willing to expose ourselves in openness to others without fear, seeing each person we meet as having a significance because both of us are accepted and loved by God . . .

To have a prayerful approach to people is to have eyes to see, a mind intent upon seeing, a heart hopeful of seeing the image of God in each person I meet, to see them in themselves and in God.

It is only when this significance has been given by us in our approach to people, when we have freed ourselves of the need to assess blame and responsibilities, that we can take them on to the next step on the road to redemption, namely, to be aware of their true selves and that which is blocking the potentialities which lie within them. It is this kind of freedom which the Christ in us brings in our personal approach: the Christ who revealed to the Samaritan woman the truths she was concealing from herself [John 4], who enabled the blind not only to see physically but to see spiritually, who enabled the prostitute to realise the real love which lay within her . . .

This will mean that in our encounters with people we shall do a great deal of listening in order that we may learn how people see themselves. By sensitivity to what is heard, and by insight into the right kind of questions to be put, we may be able both to build up the fearful and insecure and rightly disturb and undermine the complacent – those who are 'too much at ease in Zion'.

(Douglas Rhymes, 'Christ in us', from *Prayer in the Secular City*)

Discussion

Back in the same groups, participants were asked to think about their actions in a particular situation they had encountered recently, and to consider, especially in the light of the reading, anything they might have done differently.

Prayers

The prayers were offered in turn and candles were lit to accompany each person's prayer: 'We light candles to see the beauty within.'

This sharing was celebrated by sharing bread.

Reading

'Blessing the bread'
(Carter Heyward in *The New Women Included*)

Song

'Now the green blade riseth'
(*Twentieth-Century Folk Hymnal*)

The liturgy concluded with a very simple circle dance.

13

Fire, Air, Water and Earth

This liturgy originally took place in a large garden, and it lends itself to outdoor use, though this is certainly not essential. If it takes place inside, pictures to remind participants of the various natural elements may be valuable aids.

Elements

Candle
Feather
A bowl of water
A bushy twig
Bowls of earth
Sprouting shoots for planting
Materials for making collages
A bowl of fruits

Music

A taped version of the Canticle, 'Brother Sun and Sister Moon' (from Paul Winter's Missa Gaia: The Earth Mass) was used, with all joining in the chorus: 'For the beauty of the Earth, O sing today'.

Fire

The candle was lit.

Voice 1   The Holy Spirit is an unquenchable fire who bestows all excellence, sparks all worth, awakens all goodness, ignites speech, inflames humanity. Yet in this radiance is a restorative stillness. It is the stillness that is also found in the will to good. It spreads to all sides.

O Holy Spirit, Fiery Comforter Spirit, Life of the life of all creatures,
Holy are you, you that give existence to all form.
Holy are you, you that cleanse deep hurt.
Fire of love, breath of all holiness.

Air

The feather was laid down as a symbol of air.

Participants were asked to become very conscious of their breath as they inhaled and exhaled.

Voice 2   Humankind should ponder God, recognize God's wonders and signs.
The blowing wind, the mild moist air, the exquisite greening of trees and grasses.
In their beginning, in their ending, they give God their praise.
The air blowing everywhere serves all creatures. Ever is the firmament its support.
Ever is it held, carried, by the power of God. God's word is in all creation, visible and invisible.

Water

The bowl of water and bushy twig were placed centrally.

Voice 3   I adorn all the earth, I am led by the spirit to feed the purest streams.
I am the rain, coming from the dew that causes the grasses to laugh with the joy of life.
I call forth tears, the aroma of holy work. I am the yearning for good.

Participants sprinkled each other with the water, in turn round the circle. As they did this each said, 'May this water cleanse and heal you.'

Earth

The bowls of earth and the sprouting shoots were placed centrally.

Voice 4   The Earth is mother of all that is natural, mother of all that is
human.
She is the mother of all, for contained in her are the seeds of
all.
The earth of humankind contains all moistness, all verdancy,
all germinating power.
All creation comes from it. It forms not only the basic raw
material for humankind,
but also the substance for the incarnation of God's son.

Intercessions

*Shoots were planted as each person said a prayer, aloud or silently if pre-
ferred.*

*Participants divided into four groups to make collages based on one of
the four elements.*

Song

Based on the theme of the liturgy

Prayers

*On this occasion, the prayers were taken from those used at a Navajo
Catholic church, based on the idea of the four directions: the cold north,
the dawning east, the warm south, the west of the setting sun.*

Sharing of the Summer Fruits (read antiphonally)

A   We belong to one another and all creation and through this bond to
Jesus, who, on the day he handed over his freedom to those who
would abuse him, had a meal with his friends, eating and drinking
with them. So we eat together as a symbol of sharing our common
humanity.

B   We celebrate our freedom to choose, born of the breaking down of old ways. We proclaim the possibility of new life. We declare our intention to live in that hope.

A   Now we are joined together, women of faith, with all who seek God's freedom. We live and search together for a shared vision of cosmos in which all are free to enjoy God's generosity. We keep alive the memory of the crucifixion of Jesus together with his resurrection. We root the possibility of our freedom in this experience.

B   Strengthening God, take away all that prevents us achieving this. Strengthening God, take away all that prevents us achieving this. Strengthening God, give us true peace.

All   **We pray that we will be made new to live our life in the peace born of true freedom. We choose from these fruits, symbols of God's generosity.**

The bowl of fruits was passed round, with the words, 'Choose freely of the fruits of God's generosity.'

A circle dance concluded the liturgy.

14

Balance

Balance is not a static thing but a dynamic one. We should seek for it in activity and in cessation from activity. This liturgy needs sufficient space for group work and for a circle dance.

Elements

Coloured card circles
Pens
A tree branch and means of fixing the circles to it

Introduction

A piece of music suitable for creating an atmosphere of calm and reflection, shutting out all external distractions, was played.

Reading

On this occasion a poem by Helder Camara, *The Desert is Fertile* was used.

Asking for forgiveness (read round the group in turn)

Reader   O loving Creator, forgive us for not allowing ourselves time to be, nor the time to stand and stare, wondering at the glories of your creation.

All   **Send us your spirit to guide us.**

Reader   O Source of Love, forgive us for not loving ourselves enough, so that we neglect our own needs, to the detriment of others.
All   **Send us your wisdom to infuse us.**

Reader   O Caring God, forgive us for not seeking hard enough to listen to others, but yet not be swamped by their needs.
All   **Send us your Spirit of discernment.**

Reader   O Compassionate Creator, forgive us for our tendency to pass by on the other side, fearing the involvement of compassion.
All   **Help us to reflect in our lives the loving mutuality of the Trinity.**

Reader   O loving Empowerer, forgive us for not sufficiently engaging ourselves in the struggle against patriarchy and the abuse of authority, whether in Church or secular life.
All   **Send us the courage to be your prophetic witness.**

Reader   O Mother God, help us to see that there is more to mothering than physically giving birth: Enable us to understand the nurturing role of all in fostering wholeness in the life of the spirit.
All   **Enrich our sensitivity in our search for meaning.**

Reader   O God of justice and mercy, forgive us for putting our own interests, individually or nationally, above those of our sisters and brothers in developing or poor countries.
All   **Give us new understanding of the interconnectedness of all humanity.**

O living God, who intends us to live in harmony with you, with ourselves and with others, give us new hearts to strive for a balance in our lives and in our relations with our neighbours, both far and wide.

Discussion

Groups of three were formed, with each group taking a coloured card circle (marked with concentric circles and pre-cut so that they can form spirals).

Balance

Words which to group members conveyed the meaning of 'balance' were written round the circle.

A mobile was made with all the circles and hung from the tree branch.

Psalm (said antiphonally)

A   God is my strong rock in whom I trust, and all my confidence I rest in her. Deep in my mother's womb, she knew me;

B   Before my limbs were formed, she yearned for me. Each of my movements she remembers with compassion, and when I was still unseen, she did imagine me.

A   Her strength brought me forth into the light; it was she who delivered me. Hers were the hands that held me safe;

B   She cherished me upon my mother's breast.

A   When I stammer, she forms the words in my mouth, and when I am silent, she has understood my thoughts.

B   If I shout and rage, she hears my plea and my uncertainty.

A   When I am afraid, she stays close to me, and when I am full of terror, she does not hide her face.

B   If I struggle against her, she will contain me, and when I resist her, she will match my strength.

A   But if I am complacent, she confronts me;

B   When I cling to falsehood, she undermines my pride; for she is jealous for my integrity, and her longing is for nothing less than truth.

A   To all who are weak she shows compassion, and those who are downtrodden she causes to rise.

B   But she will confound the arrogant at the height of their power, and the oppressor she will throw to the ground; the strategies of the hardhearted she will utterly confute.

A   God pities the fallen, and I will love her; she challenges the mighty, and I desire her with my whole heart.

B   God is the rock in whom I put my trust, and all my meaning is contained in her; for without God there is no security, and apart from her there is no place of safety.

Reading

Ephesians 4:13–16 (Growing in Christ)

Song

'Peace is flowing like a river'

Reading

Ecclesiastes 3 (The seasons of things)

Song (sung moving in a circle)

'I'm dancing, I'm singing, I'm full of joy!'

15

Justice

The theme of justice has proved very significant to many women's groups, and it has always figured large in liturgies. Here, readings from the Bible and from other sources are used to support it.

Elements

A loaf of bread

Psalm 17

(A free version, said antiphonally)

A   Loving Creator, hear our prayer and listen to our call made in the spirit of truth.

B   You know what we are, and that we seek to be faithful to you:
We search your word to find our way.
Let us walk in your footsteps so that our feet do not slip.

A   We call on you, O Creator of life and you answer us.
Listen to our voice and show us your loving kindness,
O saviour of all who flee evil.

B   Strengthen us in the struggle to do your will.
Let our reward be to see you face to face,
And come into your loving presence.

Reading

Remember this, everyone should be quick to listen but slow to speak and slow to human anger . . . You must do what the Word tells you and not just listen to it and deceive yourselves. Anyone who listens to the Word and takes no action is like people who look at their own features in a mirror and go off and immediately forget it . . . Anyone who is wise and understanding among you should from a good life give evidence of deeds done in the gentleness of wisdom . . . the wisdom that comes down from above is essentially something pure; it is also peaceable, kindly and considerate; it is full of mercy and shows itself by doing good; nor is there any trace of partiality or hypocrisy in it. The peace sown by peacemakers brings a harvest of justice.

(James 1:19, 22–25; 3:13, 17–18)

Asking for forgiveness

A   We are called to love one another in your name, yet what have we done? We talk about love with our lips,

B   But we pass on the other side when needs press in upon us, rules matter more than compassion, the law than the spirit.

All   **Forgive us for our failure to listen to your call to show forth your love in our lives and that of the Church.**

A   We have been called to be sisters and brothers of Christ, yet what have we done? We have allowed the dominations and oppressions of the world to enter into Christ's body.

B   We have failed to listen to each other although we are all called to be a chosen race, a royal priesthood, and a consecrated nation.

All   **Send forth your spirit into our hearts so that we may truly share with one another the work of building up your realm here on earth.**

A   You created human beings in your own image, 'male and female God created them'.

B   Yet your people have treated women, made in the image of God, as inferior and defective.

All   **Help us to build up a true community of women and men in the Church, where sexual and racial discrimination is overcome.**

A   God our liberator, through Christ's redeeming act we have been made free and brought out into the light.

B   Yet we fear to act as prophets when we see that things need changing.

All Forgive us, O loving Creator, for our lack of courage. Send forth your Spirit and make your new creation truly effective in us. Help all your people to work together in love and trust to build up the body of Christ.

Reading

Blessed are you who are the lowly, the grassroots, powerless yet filled with a passion to grow and make good. You understand God's purpose.

Blessed are you many, now, who have found such depth of expression in your grief. You shall find comfort in what you have caused to change.

Blessed are you who understand that justice must be made present always. You shall see it happen in time.

Blessed are you who show compassion to those who repulse you. You shall experience compassion yourself.

Blessed are you who do not judge but see everyone with clear eyes. You see God in all creation.

Blessed are you who are peacemakers. You are my own.

Blessed are you who are excluded, suffering abuse, ridicule and scorn for what you are doing for me. To you I give my deep unstinting love.

Be happy my prophets, you are not the first, and most likely will not be the last, but I love you for what you are doing.

You are the salt of the earth, bringing integrity to my world.

You shine as a light on the world, O my people, illuminating cities, lands and continents exposing injustice.

Shine your light for all to see and understand who I am and what I ask of you, this day.

(adapted from the Beatitudes in Matthew 5)

Prayers

Silence, followed by individual intercessions.

Statement of Faith

Participants voiced for themselves and also for the group what they considered to be their most important beliefs, especially in the area of justice.

Blessing of the Bread

The bread was broken and passed round.

All   And as we break the bread we thank you, Source of all our being, for the life and knowledge of yourself which you gave to us through Jesus your child.
To you be glory for ever.
As this broken bread was scattered upon the mountains, but was brought together and became one, so let your Church be gathered together from the ends of the earth, into your kingdom, for yours is the glory and the power, through Jesus Christ for ever.

We give thanks to you, O loving Creator, for your holy name which you made to dwell in our hearts, and for the knowledge and faith and immortality which you made known to us through Jesus your child.
To you be glory for ever.

(adapted from the Agape prayers of the early Christian document, *The Didache*)

We share this loaf today, as a sign that we are all one in the body of Christ. Just as many grains came together into the one loaf, so we are all one in Christ Jesus. Help us to reflect the life giving love of the Creator, Redeemer and Spirit in all our relationships and actions.

The Peace

All held hands and sang:

'Shalom, my friends, shalom my friends, shalom, shalom;
the peace of Christ I give you today, shalom, shalom' (3 times)

Participants then greeted one another.

16

Leadership

It has often been difficult for women to assume leadership, either because within the church they have not been given the opportunity to do so, or because they have been slow to recognize in themselves the potential to do so. But leadership need not be monolithic, and women have often been happier to use a more collaborative model, such as that which is presented here.

Elements

> Stones
> Grapes
> Flowers and a bowl of water
> Two plants, one of which will not survive

Introduction

Song

'Walk in the Light'

Reading

John 15:12–15 (Love one another)

Litany on Collaborative Authority

Each person in the group read a verse, while all joined in the refrain.

Voice	O Sustainer and giver of life, free your people from the temptations of power, from the urge to control rather than enable.
All	**Come, Spirit, liberate us from the forces of domination.**
Voice	O Loving Empowerer, help us to challenge abuse of authority wherever it is to be found, including in ourselves.
All	**Come, Spirit, give us strength not to walk by on the other side.**
Voice	O Still Small Voice, help the People of God to learn to listen to each other, and those in authority to understand the strength that comes from true consultation.
All	**Come, Spirit of Understanding, deepen our insights.**
Voice	O Loving Creator, help us to affirm ourselves and others, understanding that we are all uniquely created and have a voice that needs to be heard.
All	**Come, Creator of Diversity, and help us see the value of difference.**
Voice	O God who made both women and men in your image, help your church not to deface its image by treating women as inferior beings. Help us to recognize and challenge discrimination based on sex, race, sexual orientation, clericalism and other excuses for exclusion.
All	**Come, Spirit of Equality, and imbue us with the values of inter-connectedness with all created nature, human and non-human.**
	O Loving God, lead us in your ways and breathe courage in your people so we may truly reflect in our lives the loving mutuality of the Trinity.

Readings

The readings (from Joan Chittister, *The Heart of Flesh*) *were interspersed with actions.*

What the world needs are more circles and fewer pyramids. Circles are strange and wonderful things. No one knows where a circle either begins or ends. No one can tell what is its most accomplished part. There is no up to go to in a circle, no steps to climb to arrive there, no top to get to, no crowning point upon which to plant a flag or stake a claim or build a throne . . . Ladders and pyramids assume a society of serfs, of peasants, of lackeys and underlings, of in-group and out-groups, of higher and lower classes. Circles on the other hand assume a society of equals. It isn't that circles are disorderly or chaotic; it's just that they depend more on consensus than they do on control.

Each person present took a stone as symbol of power and the group built a pyramid over a plant placed in the middle of the group, thereby squashing it.

The Active Love of God

We are asking, by the active love of God in us, to be delivered from all evil. For that to happen we must play our part: by resisting temptation; by forgiving the faults of others; by sharing our bread. These are the conditions to be fulfilled, the tasks to be carried out in the world, if the practice of God's will is to be achieved on earth as it is in heaven. Only then will God's kingdom become a reality. Only then will God's name be kept holy in the practice of our lives. Only then will we be true sisters and brothers in our creator.

(Ed O Connell, in *The Trampled Vineyard*)

Women, never part of the power structure, never confronted with ladders to climb, have always functioned extremely well in circles. They gathered in prayer circles and sewing circles and the circle of the family. They functioned without pyramids, without power, without status, often without expectation of positions of honour or institutional domination. They learned to function as one human being among many and became totally human because of it.

Each participant took a stone as a symbol of power and made a circle around the second plant, thus protecting it.

Finally the earth itself is circular, but it has been treated as a pyramid, cut up into pieces, dominated, destroyed and doomed to struggle for its own existence and the survival of those who depend on it but live under the philosophy of the pyramid. Circles bind the human race together, pyramids separate it into layers of humanity, one level standing on the backs of another.

Intercessions

As each person voiced her own prayer, she took one of the flowers already provided and placed it in a bowl of water.

Poem (said antiphonally)

I dream of a church
That joins in with God's laughing
As she rocks in her rapture,
Enjoying her art:
She's glad of her world,
In its risking and growing:
'tis the child she has borne
and holds close to her heart.

I dream of a church
That joins in with God's weeping
As she crouches, weighed down
By the sorrow she sees:
She cries for the hostile,
The cold and no-hoping,
For she bears in herself
Our despair and dis-ease.

I dream of a church that
Joins in with God's dancing
As she moves like the wind
And the wave and the fire
A church that can pick up
Its skirts, pirouetting,
With the steps that can signal
God's deepest desire.

I dream of a church that
Joins in with God's loving
As she bends to embrace
The unlovely and the lost.
A church that can free,
By its sharing and daring,

The imprisoned and poor,
And then shoulder the cost.

God, make us a church
That joins in with your living
As you cherish and challenge,
Rein in and release,
A church that is winsome,
Impassioned, inspiring:
Lioness of your justice
And lamb of your peace.

(Kate Compston, 'I dream of a church' in *Network*, 58, 1999)

Agape

The grapes were shared.

All   **We now share the fruit of the vine. These grapes, just as they are one bunch yet many fruits, so we too are brought together and are one though many. As the grapes are passed round, say, 'May this sign of our unity strengthen you on your journey.'**

The Peace

Holding hands, all sang:

'Shalom my friends'

17

A 'Wilderness' Liturgy

This liturgy was improvised when the planner for the evening was ill, and additionally the kitchen attached to the room where the liturgy took place was unavailable, so it was impossible to make cups of tea afterwards. The liturgy shows that detailed planning is not always necessary.

Elements

A sufficient number of small objects for everyone to have at least one each: the selection will depend on what is easily found – an ornament, a fossil, a picture, a notebook, a purse, a paperclip, a toy, a scarf, are all possibilities.
A candle
A loaf of bread
A glass of water

Introduction

N. had prepared a liturgy for us but at the last minute she is unable to come. The kitchen is being redecorated and so we have to improvise. We could feel abandoned and shut out. We are in some sense in a wilderness, but we should make the best of it, and start by lighting a candle of joy and hope.

The candle was lit, and people were invited to make their selection of the objects brought. They were then asked to step forward in turn, say their names and the reason why they have chosen a specific object, and then to place it near the candle.

Discussion (in pairs or threes)

Do you ever feel on the outside, marginalized, ostracized?

Readings

Poems about a woman silenced and about the importance of words, from Amanda Hopkinson, *Lovers and Comrades: Women's Resistance Poetry*: 'Prologue' by Luz de la Vega, and 'Reflection' by Janina Fernandez

Discussion

Ideas about these poems were exchanged within the whole group.

Being in the wilderness can provide the opportunity for a new direction, new beginnings. Please speak if you wish about any such hopes for yourself you may have.

The bread and water were shared, with the words: 'Unless the bread is broken, it cannot be shared,' and 'More than food in the wilderness, we need water.'

Prayers

Everyone who chose to do so said her own bidding prayer. These prayers were followed by a group prayer.

'Tender God, touch us'
(Carter Heyward in *Celebrating Women*)

18

Anger and Peace

Anger is not an emotion that we should be afraid or ashamed of. Rather we should ensure that it is expressed, possibly in symbolic form, and not repressed in a way that will lead to resentment building up. In this liturgy, art is used as a way of symbolizing anger.

Elements

> Materials for making a collage
> Candles
> Stones
> Suitable music

Reading

Today has been a restless day
things going wrong in all directions
and my anger is rising
at others, at circumstances, at myself.

God, you are in the midst of this
I sense your presence
prowling like a tiger pushing me, pursuing me,
restless yourself until I change.

I am ready to let rip
to hurl stones into oceans
to pound my fists into a brick wall
I am ready to shout

to rip sheets into darkness
to bury my head into warm flesh and sob

I am afraid, God
that there is no one here but you and me
my friends are out or busy or far away.
Do I trust you enough to give you my anger, my loneliness?
Do I believe you enough to reach through the emptiness
and grasp for your hand?

Credo
God, I love you,
I can say no other words.

(Ruth Burgess, 'Credo' in *Pushing the Boat Out*)

Short silence

Readings

I tell you, unless your sense of justice surpasses that of the religious
scholars and the Pharisees, you will not enter the kingdom of heaven.
You've heard that our ancestors were told, 'No killing' and 'Every
murderer will be subject to judgment.' But I tell you that everyone who
is angry with sister or brother is subject to judgment; anyone who says
to sister or brother, 'I spit in your face!' will be subject to the Sanhedrin;
and anyone who vilifies them with name-calling will be subject to the
fires of Gehenna. If you bring your gift to the altar and there remember
that your sister or brother has a grudge against you, leave your gift there
at the altar. Go to be reconciled to them, and then come and offer your
gift.

(Matthew 5:21–6)

Mark 11:15–18 (Jesus cleanses the temple)

Discussion (in pairs or threes)

When is anger justified? What are the best ways of dealing with negative
feelings? Are there constructive approaches to the problem?

A collage expressing anger was made.

135

Reading

> I was angry with my friend:
> I told my wrath, my wrath did end.
> I was angry with my foe:
> I told it not, my wrath did grow.
>
> And I water'd it in fears,
> Night and morning with my tears;
> And I sunned it with my smiles,
> And with soft deceitful wiles.
>
> And it grew both day and night,
> Till it bore an apple bright;
> And my foe beheld it shine,
> And he knew that it was mine,
>
> And into my garden stole
> When the night had veil'd the pole:
> In the morning glad I see
> My foe outstretch'd beneath the tree.
> (William Blake, 'The Poison Tree')

Prayers

Each person made her intercession, aloud or silently, either lighting a candle or laying down a stone in a pile.

Song (tune: Lord of all hopefulness)

> Peace flowing outward and peace flowing in,
> Draw peace from the centre in which we begin;
> Find peace in the ending, the close of the day,
> Let peace in the heart wipe the evil away.
>
> Strength flowing outward and strength flowing in,
> Draw strength from the centre in which we begin;
> Find strength in the ending, the close of the day;
> Let strength in the heart wipe the evil away.

Anger and Peace

Hope flowing outward . . .

Joy flowing outward . . .

Love flowing outward. . .
(June Boyce-Tillman)

19

A Shared Meal

A long tradition, beginning with the Passover meal in the Hebrew scriptures and continuing through the Last Supper, has associated meals with worship. Many women's liturgies include a sharing of food; this one places greater emphasis on the meal aspect. This liturgy was carried out with a separate space where the food was originally put. This would not have to be a separate room, however. A table and chairs were needed, so that participants could reflect prayerfully about food.

Elements

> Food brought by participants
> A loaf of bread
> Candles

On arrival participants took items of food for the meal into the kitchen. They then gathered in another room where there was a table.

Introduction

The theme was that of sharing food together; making connections with those involved in the sowing and harvesting, the preparation and the economics. Cooking connects us with friends; our memories; tasting another person's culture. Food is also a means of communication – eucharist, sharing meals as Jesus did.

Song

'God has a table'
(*Heaven Shall Not Wait*, Vol. 1)

A Shared Meal

The group divided into four to give four voices. During the song, participants went into the kitchen, brought food, plates and cutlery out and laid the table together. Remaining standing, they named themselves.

Litany

'Blessing the bread' (read in four voices)
(Carter Heyward in *The New Women Included*)

Discussion

Shared reflection on the food. What is it made from? Who made it?

Bread was broken, shared and eaten.

Silence

Poem

'Come to this table'
(Jan Berry in *Bread of Tomorrow*)

Prayers

These were said, aloud or silently, while the candles were lit.

Participants ate together, telling stories to each other: stories around food, meals – funny, sad, ordinary.

Thanksgiving and Departure

A suitable prayer at this point would be:

Glory to God our Creator, to Jesus our redeemer, and to the Spirit who gives us life.
As it was in the beginning, is now, and ever shall be, world without end.

Alternatively, a verse from a hymn, said or sung, or Psalm 134, 'Bless the Lord, all you who serve God', could be used.

Song

'God has a table'

While this was sung, the table was cleared and everything taken back into the kitchen.

Dismissal and Blessing

20

Facing Change

This liturgy gives particular attention to the kind of skills and communication needed in today's society, and the way in which this may cause anxiety to many people.

Elements

> Bricks or similar objects
> Oil for anointing
> Fruit
> Bread

Readings

Non-scriptural readings were taken from the Church of England Board for Social Responsibility publication, *Cybernauts Awake!*

Introduction

Words about the theme of the liturgy by way of introduction.

Prayer (said antiphonally)

A Come, be with us, for we are here to create,
B To create, as Jesus witnessed women creating,
A Taking bushels of wheat, bushels of raw humanity,
B Adding the yeast of their womanhood,
A Working it in, kneading, kneading, labouring

B   To make it penetrate the substance of the raw wheat
A   To manufacture, to create the bread
B   That in turn will help to nourish, to sustain the life of the world.
A   We are here to create a new world:
B   A new world by our humble efforts,
A   In themselves as puny as those of the Jewish bakerwoman
B   Whom we know as creatrix,
      In whom you have made visible your creative power.
A   Give us, Creator Spirit, a vision of the world
B   As your love would make it.
A   Help us create a world where women are esteemed
B   And all the weak and poor appreciated.
A   Help us create a world where the benefits of culture
B   Are shared equally between men and women,
A   Between races and nations.
B   Help us to create a world where peace is laced
A   With justice, and justice intertwined with love.
B   And help us, Creator supreme, to create a church
A   Where all who share human life will recognize
B   In themselves and in others the one image of yourself
A   In which they were conceived.
B   Help us by the inspiration of your Spirit
      To build this world – this Church. **Amen.**

(Sr Kira Sohldoost)

Reading

'Neighbourliness'
(from *Cybernauts Awake!*)

Prayer

Be thou my guardian
at the switching on of my computer.
Protect me from all harmful rays.
Guide my fingers as they move across the keyboard
Be thou the inspiration of my heart.
Close watch the keys as I travel across the internet.

Facing Change

Guard me from the sites that can cause harm.
Keep me patient when good matter is downloading
and guide me to avoid a waste of time.
Thy blessing rest upon the system
from clicking mouse to printer hardware.
Be thou the good sustainer of the software.
May beauty be the output of us all.

(Sara Ingles)

Prayer

Facing change (said antiphonally)

A   We are your pilgrim people, Lord, yet we fear to leave the trodden path.
All   Come, Spirit, embolden us to embrace change.

B   Help us, O Creator God, to abandon outworn ways of thinking and re-envisage the meaning of life.
All   Come, Spirit of truth, give us the power of discernment of the way ahead.

A   Loving Christ, we are called to walk in your footsteps yet we falter on the way.
All   Send your spirit to infuse us with your generosity and courage.

B   We find it hard to stand out against current false values
All   Come, Spirit of renewal, inspire us to work for change.

A   Let us rejoice in all that God has done for us.
All   May our hearts be open to joy.
Let us face the future with anticipation not fear.
May we be prepared to sow seeds but not be anxious about the reaping. May we be thankful for our families, networks and communities but also use our gifts for those beyond.

Chant

'O Lord hear my prayer' (Taizé)

The participants placed bricks on the ground in a circle, making an intercession that focused on how we identify changes in our lives and what help we need to manage change.

Poem (read antiphonally)

'Going over'
(Kathy Galloway in *Love Burning Deep*)

Each person anointed the next with oil, saying 'I anoint you with oils to help you on this journey through change.'

Prayer

'Spirit of Integrity'
(Janet Morley in *The New Women Included*)

Sharing

All   O loving Creator, bless this fruit and bread, symbols of the abundance with which you endowed us and strengthen in us the quality of fruitfulness in the way we live our lives.

Fruit and bread were passed round, with the words, 'This is fruit/bread to refresh and sustain you.'

Final Prayer

Iona Blessing: 'Come Lord Jesus be our Guest'

21

Journeying

There are many times when we feel that there is no stability in our life. Liturgy, by recognizing that we are pilgrims on a journey, can help us cope with this feeling. This liturgy took place in a garden, but any setting where movement from place to place is possible would be suitable.

Elements

A number of pebbles (These should include one that has particular significance; in this instance, a stone from the Sea of Galilee was used, but one with an interesting shape or colour could equally be substituted.)
Flowers
A loaf of bread
Coloured string (A labyrinth was laid out in advance.)

Introduction

As participants introduced themselves, they passed the stone from the Sea of Galilee to each speaker in turn.

Reading

God has created me,
God is my Lord, having dominion over me.
God is also my strength,
for I can wish to do nothing good without God.
Through God I have living spirit,
Through God I have life and movement,

Through God I learn, I find my path.
If I call in truth this God directs my steps,
setting my feet to the rhythm of God's precepts.
I run like a deer that seeks its spring.
(Hildegard of Bingen)

Sharing

In pairs, participants discussed with each other where they felt they were on the journey.

Prayer

A prayer was said which recalled the dance of creation and the way in which God's spirit dances within us. The patterns of a dance recall the way in which we are constantly meeting and becoming involved with each other.

Circle Dance of Journeying

Participants moved to another part of the garden.

On the way they were anointed, each person doing so asking for strength for the journey.

A labyrinth had been previously prepared, marked out with coloured string. One person spoke briefly about its significance and then each person in turn walked the labyrinth, picking up a pebble at the start. This was laid down in a container in the centre, symbolizing laying down burdens and difficulties. A flower was then taken in its place. Steps were retraced, and in this 'journey' the next person coming to the centre was passed on the way. After all had had their turn, participants returned to the part of the garden where the liturgy began, humming the tune of 'Lord of all hopefulness', which is the melody of the next song.

Song (tune: Lord of all hopefulness)

'Peace flowing outward and peace flowing in'
(June Boyce-Tillman)

Journeying

Subsequent verses begin 'Hope flowing outward', 'Joy flowing outward', 'Love flowing outward'

Prayers

Participants laid down their flowers on the central table as they prayed, speaking their prayer or saying it silently, as preferred.

Sharing

The bread was broken by each in turn, passing it to the next person saying, 'The bread of sustenance for your journey.' Before eating, all said the blessing:

All   We share this loaf today, as a sign that we are all one in the body of Christ. Just as many grains came together into the one loaf, so we are all one in Christ Jesus. Help us to reflect the life giving love of the Creator, Redeemer and Spirit in all our relationships and actions.

Song

Deep peace of the running wave to you,
Deep peace of the silent stars to you,
Deep peace of the flowing air to you,
Deep peace of the quiet earth to you.
May peace, may peace, may peace fill your soul,
Let peace, let peace, let peace make you whole.

WOMEN

22

Reclaiming Mary

The context of this liturgy was a conference organized by St Joan's Alliance in 1988 on rethinking about Mary, where the theologian Mary Grey gave a paper on reclaiming Mary. A few changes have been made to this liturgy since then.

Elements

A selection of pictures (postcards, prints, etc.) depicting Mary
Pebbles
Flowers and a vase
Bread and wine

Song

'Where are you bound Mary?'
(*Celebration Hymnal*)

Reading

When Mary visits her cousin Elizabeth, she does not become enraptured because she is pregnant. On the contrary she glorifies God's liberating action precisely because she is herself the liberated Israel . . . Mary's task was to continue God's liberating activity in the world. The last shall be first and those who rule must, on their way to the kingdom, join the ranks of the poor, whose head and example is Mary.

(Catherina Halkes, 'Mary and Women' in *Concilium* issue *Mary and the Churches*)

Short silence

Discussion (in pairs or threes)

The significance of Mary to us personally

Choosing Pictures

A selection of visual images of Mary was placed on the floor and one or two were chosen by each participant. After a few moments for silent thought, those who wished to do so talked about their personal choice of picture.

Readings

Voice 1   Mary is the prophetic and liberating Woman of the people. 'All the theological greatness of Mary is based on the lowliness of her historical tradition.' She is Mary of Nazareth, a woman of the people, who observed the usual customs of her day, visited her relatives, took part in wedding celebrations and worried about her son, following him even to the foot of the cross, as any mother would do. 'Because of this ordinariness and not in spite of it, God did "great things" for her.'

Leader   O loving and sustaining God, help us to challenge the powerful and work to empower all so that they may use their gifts in building up your realm.

All   **Magnificat** (sung response: Taizé)

Voice 2   Mary is the perfect example of faith responding to God. She did not understand the full extent of the mystery to be brought about through her but she trusted in God and concerned herself with others – her cousin Elizabeth, her son lost on pilgrimage, the guests with no wine. 'Persons can be liberators only if they free themselves from their own preoccupations and place their lives at the service of others.'

Leader   Help us, O loving and sustaining Creator, to be as responsive to your word as Mary was, and to identify ourselves with the needs of others, particularly women who have suffered so much by the distortion of your word.

All	**Magnificat**

Voice 3   Thirdly, she is the prophetess of the Magnificat who anticipated the liberating proclamation of her son and was attentive to the fate of the poor and marginalized: she invoked 'divine revolution in the relationship between oppressors and oppressed'.

Leader   O loving and sustaining Redeemer, help us to live out the Magnificat in our attitudes and actions.

All   **Magnificat**

Voice 4   Finally, in Latin-American popular religion, Mary is seen as the champion of the poor. The masses bring their troubles to the centres of Marian pilgrimage where they are filled with renewed strength and hope to carry on struggling and surviving.

All   **O loving and sustaining Spirit, inspire us to free the Image of Mary, Mother of God, from the pious distortions of the ages, and find in her a model of challenge and hope.**

(Based on Leonardo and Clodovis Boff, *Introducing Liberation Theology*)

Building the Cairn

Each person took one or two pebbles, which they placed in the form of a cairn in the middle of the group. This was seen as either laying down the burden of a distorted image of Mary or of a mother/child relationship, or as a building up of a hope for the future. Participants either spoke about what the pebbles represented or placed them on the heap in silence.

Song (tune: Quem Pastores)

Mary, chosen to be mother
Of a child in myst'ry hidden,
Not o'ercome by fear or terror,
Teach us how to persevere.

Mary, wandr'ing through the desert,
Trav'lling on uncertain, anxious,
Held by arms, supporting, loving,
Teach us how to persevere.

Mary, reaching Bethl'em's safety,
Resting in a place so lowly,
Giving birth in painful hoping,
Teach us how to persevere.

Mary, dreaming of a future
When her son would grow to manhood,
Loving, trusting, planning, hoping,
Teach us how to persevere.

(June Boyce-Tillmann, *In Praise of All Encircling Love*, Vol. 1)

Magnificat

All   O compelling God, announcing your presence not among the mighty but in obscurity.
You move us with a compulsion to acknowledge the injustice in our midst,
To reject the structures and attitudes that discriminate and to bring insight and change to those in positions of dominance.
Send your transfiguring spirit to overshadow us, removing the obstructing divisive shadow of prejudice and ignorance which clouds the vision of your Church.
Make us worthy witnesses, as Mary in the transforming work you have planned.
Give us energy and determination in our choosing to co-operate with you through Jesus Christ incarnate.

(Lala Winkley)

Intercessions

During the prayers, flowers were placed in the vase.

Leader   Mary was prepared to fly in the face of social custom in her 'Yes' to God. We too need courage to stand out against patriarchal mindsets and reclaim liberation for ourselves. As we place the flowers we have here in the vase, we can silently or aloud pray about aspects of liberation.

Blessing of Food and Drink

Leader   Blessed are you, O Lord our God, creator of this food and drink that we share together as a sign of your kingdom, which is to come in glory, and yet is already here now in so far as you live among us in the love we have for one another.

The wine was poured out.

All   **We give thanks to you, our creator, for this wine, remembering Israel your people, brought like a vine out of Egypt, and planted in the promised land.**

The wine was passed round and drunk.

The bread was then broken and passed round.

All   **As we break the bread we thank you, O Creator, for the life and knowledge of yourself which you gave us through Jesus Christ.**
To you be glory for ever.

As this broken bread was scattered upon the mountains but was brought together and became one, so let your children be gathered together from the ends of the earth into your kingdom, for yours is the glory and the power, through Jesus Christ for ever.

(from the Agape prayers of the early Christian document, *The Didache*)

All ate.

23

Reclaiming Mary Magdalene

Women have often suffered from the fact that Mary Magdalene, the first apostle of the resurrection, apostle to the apostles, has traditionally been viewed as a prostitute, something for which there is no scriptural foundation. This liturgy attempts to reclaim her image.

Elements

A selection of false visual images of Mary Magdalene
Bread and wine
A metal wastepaper bin and matches

Introduction

Song (sung or spoken)

'Judas and Mary'
(Sydney Carter in *The Present Tense*, Vol. 1)

and/or

Reading

John 12:1–8 (Mary anoints Jesus)

Leader   Who is the Mary in this song (or reading)? Is it Mary Magdalene?

Group members made suggestions.

Leader   There are a number of women called Mary in the New Testament and some of these have been confused, not only with each other but with other women briefly mentioned in the Gospels.

By conflating different accounts, the individual called Mary Magdalene has been mistakenly identified with a number of other women, notably in the accounts of women who anointed Jesus, and in particular with the unnamed woman 'who had a bad name in the town', in Luke 7:36. Modern scholarship holds that there is no justification for identifying the sinful woman with Mary Magdalene, who appears in the next chapter (8:2), where she is shown as having been healed from possession by seven devils (most likely to have been mental illness) and as accompanying Jesus along with other women and the twelve men.

The mistake confusing the various women does not appear until the fourth century but since then, reinforced by Gregory the Great's advocacy, it has been a powerful force.

But what do we know of the biblical Mary Magdalene? Apart from her healing and accompanying Jesus, we find her given a place of pre-eminence among the women at the foot of the cross (Matthew 27:56; Mark 15:40; John 19:25), at the burial (Matthew 27:61) and at the appearances on Easter day (Luke 24:10; Matthew 28:1; Mark 16:1–9; John 20:1–18), where Mary Magdalene is not portrayed as anointing the living Christ but going to the tomb to anoint the dead body of her Lord.

Let other voices tell us their insights.

Readings

Voice 1   Elisabeth Moltmann Wendell in *The Women around Jesus* believes that those who love the biblical Mary Magdalene, and compare her with the 'Christian' tradition of Mary Magdalene must get very angry. She points out that even today most Christians believe that Mary Magdalene is the 'great sinner'. Western literature and art are full of stories and pictures of the beautiful repentant woman. The woman in

Luke 7, and Mary Magdalene who appears in all four Gospels, have as little common identity as Peter and Judas.

Moltmann Wendell goes on to speak about Mary Magdalene's experience in the garden, when being told not to touch her risen Lord was a great shock. She was no longer experiencing 'the tender, friendly Jesus'. It is not possible for her to touch him, he cannot be brought back and held. Mary Magdalene may no longer spontaneously throw her arms around him, yet she clings to him because her previous relationship with him has fallen apart.

Moltmann Wendell writes that she would prefer to translate the words, 'Don't touch me' as an appeal to 'Grow up! Be mature! Accept the grief of parting.'

Voice 2   In the South African artist Dinah Cormick's examination of over four hundred visual images of Mary Magdalene, she found that the overwhelming emphasis has been the ignoring of scripture and the concentration on Mary Magdalene as a supposed repentant sexual sinner, often using erotic imagery. She writes in her conclusion:

'The Church has utilized the visual imagery of Mary Magdalene to diminish the most favoured disciple of Christ. The missionary role has been undermined, her covenantal call disregarded. Instead the patriarchal Church has nourished and promoted the portrayal of (her) as the repentant sinner . . .

'The imagery proclaims an unfair notion that women are inherently sinful and in continuous need of repentance. This interpretation of a woman solely within a sexual context is a narrow viewpoint. For it ignores the holistic perception of her worth and experience as a thinking, feeling human being, the theological implications of this visual imagery lend support to the negative attitude the Church has towards women . . .

'The visual portrayal of Mary Magdalene in Christian art has failed to do her justice. The underlying message of this visual portrayal is that women are not fit to be direct disciples of Christ in the Church . . . (yet) it is Mary Magdalene who remains at the foot of the cross. It was she who returns to the tomb at the break of the following day. It was she alone, who first recognizes the risen Christ. Chosen from among the disciples, Mary Magdalene is commissioned by Jesus to proclaim the keynote phrase in the Christian mystery, 'He is risen'.

(from Dinah Cormick's unpublished MA thesis,
Mary Magdalene: a case study in feminist ethical issues)

Sheets of false visual images were passed round the circle. Each participant took one and when all had received a copy they were torn in two, placed in a metal bin and set alight.

Song

'A Woman in her Grief'
(*In Praise of All Encircling Love*, Vol. 1)

1.
A woman in her grief
Within a garden cried
Lost in a sense of deep bereavement,
For the man she loved had died.

2.
She wandered through the paths
To search out where he lay,
In devotion, bringing spices
Her great debt to him to pay.

3.
A man in working clothes
Was also in that place;
But her loss was overwhelming
And she did not know his face.

4.
He gently said one word,
He called her by her name,
It was just the sound she longed for
And her heart was set aflame.

5.
She recognized her love
Who told her not to stay;
So she left her contemplation
For the world of everyday.

6.
At times, God you seem so close
But help us not to cling.
May such ecstasy be harnessed
For the world's transfiguring.

Reading

John 20:1–18 (Mary Magdalene at the empty tomb)

Discussion (in pairs or threes)

What was happening between Jesus and Mary Magdalene in the Garden? Some translate 'Do not touch me' as 'Do not cling to me'.

Poem

'Blessed be God for the faithfulness of Mary'
(Nicola Slee, *Easter Garden*)

This poem recalls how Mary Magdalene, having seen all the suffering of Jesus, still kept faith and came to share in the glory of his resurrection.

Discussion (in pairs or threes)

What are we clinging to that we need to give up?

Intercessions

Sharing of Bread and Wine

All   **As the bread that is scattered on the hillside**
     Was gathered together and made one,
     So too, we your people,
     Scattered through the world,
     Are gathered together around your table
     And become one.

The bread was broken and passed round; all ate the bread together.

All   **As grapes grown in the field,**
     Are gathered together and pressed into wine,
     So too are we drawn together
     And pressed by our times to share a common lot
     And are transformed into your life-blood for all.

The wine was poured and each drank in turn.

24

Honouring Our Foremothers:
A Celebratory Dinner

The occasion for this liturgy was a celebration of ten years of a women's group. Before the actual liturgy started, the meal had been prepared and various courses were brought through at different stages in the liturgy. Another part of the preparation was that each person present made a 'tablemat' by painting or decorating a paper plate in a symbolic way to commemorate her chosen 'foremother'.

Elements

Paper plates and material to decorate them
Space to display them (for instance on wall)
Candles
Food, including bread, pasta, olives, milk, honey cake, fruits, and prepared fish and vegetarian dishes
Wine

The candles were lit.

Introduction

Welcome to this dinner which is one of our ways of celebrating ten years of our organization. We celebrate with our foremothers remembered in these mats we have made. These we will name but we remember too the countless unnamed women who have gone before us.

Each person named her own name and her foremother's name.

Prayer

All   Spirit of life, we remember today the women named and unnamed, throughout time, who have used the power and gifts you gave them to change the world. We call upon our foremothers to help us discern within ourselves your power and the way to use it to bring justice to all women.

Song

'Women of power, women of struggle, we remember'

Readings

Voice 1   A reading from Exodus 3:7–8: And Yahweh said 'I have seen the miserable state of my people. I have heard their appeal to be free. Yes, I am well aware of their sufferings. I mean to deliver them and bring them to a land rich and broad, a land where milk and honey flow.'

Voice 2   We are going on a journey, a journey into the wilderness but remembering that promise. We are sustained on the journey just as the Israelites were. We have our manna: bread and olives. While eating, you might share with your neighbour your own or your foremother's experience of wilderness.

Bread and olives were passed round and eaten.

Song (sung as a round)

'Forgotten women, women of the wilderness, we proclaim you'

Voice 3   We tell our foremothers' stories while eating together, to remind one another of their variety and beauty. The bread we eat links us through time to women all over the world, the makers and breakers of bread.

Each woman held up the name of her foremother and said a few sentences about her. At the same time the pasta and bread was passed round.

Song (sung as a round, while people changed their places)

'Women of power, women of struggle, we remember'

Voice 2
Luke 24:13–35 (The road to Emmaus)

After the story, some bread was broken, and there was a reflection for two or three minutes on fish as a eucharistic symbol, led by one of the participants. The fish and vegetarian dish were then eaten.

Song (sung as a round)

'Gospel-telling women, understanding women, we remember'

Everyone moved again, plates were cleared and small plates distributed.

Voice 1   Fruit is a symbol of the gifts of women.

Each person placed a piece of fruit in the bowl, saying: 'I believe in the gifts of women.' The bowl of fruit was passed along the table, each person taking a piece of fruit and giving it to her neighbour saying, 'Stay fruitful.'

Prayer

All   We are on a journey to bring justice and liberation to all the women of the world. We have a vision that the struggles of our foremothers will not be in vain. We dream dreams for our daughters and granddaughters, that they may stand upright and strong in their lives and work.

Song (sung as a round)

'Daughters of the future, stand up with your sisters, we dream for you'

Voice 1   Remembering the promise at the start of our journey today, we offer you the milk of solidarity and the honey of sisterhood. May our organization continue to be a place to find that sustenance which is both food for the journey and at the same time the Promised Land.

The bowl of milk and the honey cake were passed round.

Prayer

All   Come, Holy Spirit, bless us as we bless each other and lead us to places we would rather not go.
Expand the horizons of our imaginations; awaken in us dangerous dreams of a new tomorrow.
Rekindle in our hearts the fire of prophetic enthusiasm, so that our group may continue to be a sacred place where God and women meet.
We are carriers of a new vision that is the Trinity's dream for us to be creative, loving and free.
We are called to be women of the gospel, committed to conversion in our effort to become a community of disciples, who live simply, love tenderly and act justly.

Litany

Leader   Let us celebrate our foremothers whose history we reclaim as we seek to create a new humanity:
All   **Remember us today.**

This response was repeated after each invocation.

Miriam, who led the slaves from Egypt into freedom:
Deborah, who judged with truth and righteousness:
Hulda, the prophet and Bruria, the rabbi:
Mary Magdalene, Apostle to the Apostles, bringer of
    of the resurrection:
Phoebe, the deacon and Priscilla and Thecla, apostles:
Catherine of Siena, who called popes and kings to repent:
Julian of Norwich, mystic of God our Mother:
Mary Ward and Julie Billiart and all the others who
    brought education to women, rich and poor:

Honouring Our Foremothers: A Celebratory Meal

Teresa of Avila and Thérèse of Lisieux, doctors of the Church:
Ita Ford, Maura Clark, Dorothy Kazal and Jean Donovan,
    who gave their lives for the poor of El Salvador:
[*Other invocations may be added at choice*]
    And all those who have worked so that women may be given
    their rightful place in the church and in society:

All   Remember us today.

Song (sung as a round, during a circle dance)

'Come Spirit circle us, fill us with hope, keep love alive'

25

'Croning': Celebrating a
Seventieth Birthday

A crone has in the past been one of many derogatory terms for an age-ing woman. Women today are reclaiming this name as one denoting the wisdom of the older woman. This liturgy was devised for a seventieth birthday celebration; aspects need to be individualized to make it appropriate to the person who is being celebrated.

Elements

    Candles
    A cloak
    A cake
    Oil for anointing

Naming

Each person round the circle gave her name.

Lighting of the Candles (one for each decade passed)

The first is for her immersion into life and the Church;
The second for her acceptance of the way people are;
The third for her sharing of herself and all that she has;
The fourth for being ever open to the wind of the spirit of change;
The fifth for her many friendships;
The sixth for her ministry and priesthood;
The seventh for her participation in death through the loss of relatives, friends [and especially her husband].

'Croning': Celebrating a Seventieth Birthday

Song

On the theme of friendship [*On this occasion, the song had been specially written by a member of the group.*]

Prayer

All We call on Sophia, the Spirit of Wisdom, to be here with us at this time when we celebrate the seventy years of life and work of our dear friend. We have lit the seven candles, one for each decade of her life. She has seen many changes in the world, in the Church and has willingly shared all that she has learned and all that she has. In the words of the Book of Wisdom: 'She deploys her strength, ordering all things for good.'

Discussion (in pairs or threes for five or ten minutes)

What unexpected thing has happened to you in your last decade?
What hope of change for yourself have you in your next decade?

Reading

(A version of Ecclesiastes chapter 3, adapted to reflect the life of the person being croned)

There is a season, a time appropriate for everything that happens under heaven;
A time to be born and called by name;
A time to be nurtured in love and encouragement;
A time for flowering in study and a time for growth in learning;
A time for opportunity in work, a re-locating that has constant recall in experience;
A time for being one and a time for joining up in that special bond of two;
A time for mothering offspring and offsprings' offspring;
A time for teaching the young;
A time for learning yet another language;
A time for archiving irreplaceable documents;
A time for gathering a library of unique radical warmth

And a time for associating in a language where women are also seen in
   God's image;
A time for planting a garden and a time for picnicking in that garden;
A time for writing and a time for editing what must be pruned;
A time for making a pastoral presence and a time which we hold in
   symbol of reform;
A time for deep sorrow in parting and a time for celebrating in song;
A dance of what has been and of how blessed is this hour of Jubilee;
A time for consolation in the close bond of friendship.
Now is the time of feeling uplifted in the mutual support of sisterhood.
The greatest wish our God has for us is to be happy and live our lives to
   the full.
This joy is bequeathed to enhance her innate wisdom which we do
   honour now.

(Lala Winkley)

Cloaking the Crone

*All held up the croning-cloak, bequeathed to women of wisdom and
long standing, above the celebrant's head.*

All   **We honour you and call you crone.**

The cloak was lowered to enfold her.

Words of Wisdom from the Crone

Song

*The Crone was then anointed with a birthday wish by each person in
turn.*

The cake was shared.

Lighting of the Eighth Candle

*The eighth candle – for the Crone's next decade – was lit. Then all laid
hands on her and said:*

May a blessing rich in power and love enfold you; spreading deep into you this day, bringing you joy. Amen.

May God fill your heart with love, your mind with peace and your body with good health. Amen.

May you continue to have courage to face the good times and the bad, and wisdom to understand and continue to grow in this next decade of your life. Amen.

We ask these blessings on you, in the name of God our Creator, Jesus our Redeemer and Sophia Spirit resting on you. Amen.

Closing Prayer

God, help us to be ever conscious of your love towards us, so that we may more faithfully work towards true communion with each other. Inspire us to play our part in the creation of a world in which all will live in your love.

The celebration ended with a circle dance.

26

Menstruation and Menopause

Menstruation has often been regarded as a subject 'not talked about in polite company'. Additionally, in many cultures, having a monthly period was one of the factors which rendered a woman ritually unclean (together with the time immediately after childbirth, for instance). It is therefore important to reclaim all parts of women's lives as suitable for liturgies.

Elements

A centrepiece based on the colour red, made from succulent red flowers and fruit
Coloured tissues
Picture reflecting women's exclusion

Introduction

Each woman said her name and named a colour that expressed her feelings at that moment.

Prayer (said all together)

'Did the woman say'
(Frances Croake Frank in *Celebrating Women*)

Leader Blood is our life-line, the thread of life which runs from conception onwards. In blood we are born, through blood we come to adulthood, through the end of bleeding we enter the third phase of life and gain a freedom. In death blood ceases, dries up and is no more.

But as the poem of Frances Croake Frank tells so eloquent-
ly, that bleeding can be a source of repression of women. Men
have always had fear of it. We ourselves may feel ambiguous
about it (it is often called the curse) but it is how women are
and how we were created by God so tonight we are having a
liturgy on menstruation. So the centrepiece is round and red
and has succulent red fruits.

Discussion (in pairs or threes for about ten minutes)

Exchange a memory of the onset of menstruation and your feelings
around menstruation.

*Each person then took a piece of coloured tissue and placed it in the
centre, saying any words they felt appropriate as they wished.*

Reading

Leviticus 12:1–8 and 15:19–30 (Ritual impurity)

*A photograph of women being excluded from a religious ceremony was
passed round.*

Leader   Leviticus is still alive even in our world.

Reading

Mark 5:21–43 (The woman with the issue of blood)

Discussion

Group reflection on the reading from Mark's Gospel.

Leader   Some of us may have arrived at menopause, or have had
premature menopause through a hysterectomy. That can be a
source of great sadness for some women. Others may welcome
it. But all of us, given normal lifespan, will have to go through
the menopause, which also has its difficulties.

Discussion (in pairs or threes)

What are your feelings about the menopause?
What benefits do you think it brings?

There was an opportunity for anyone who wished to say something in full circle.

Reading (together)

'Phenomenal Woman' by Maya Angelou

(This expresses contentment and pride in being a woman, a 'phenomenal woman'.)

Fruits were then shared, each person saying to the next woman, 'You are a phenomenal woman, God's special creation.'

Leader   Let us go out as the phenomenal women we are!
All   **Amen.**

Song

'You can't kill the Spirit'
(*The New Women Included*)

27

Mothering and Nurturing

The theme of mothering does not seem to figure very often in women's liturgies, perhaps as a reaction against too much stereotyping of women as mothers. The liturgy that follows was intended to emphasize that mothering involves much more than the physical aspects, and many people provide mothering and nurturing, often without themselves being aware of doing so.

Elements

A tape or CD with music
A candle
Small stones
A wastepaper basket or small bin
A bowl of water and flower heads
Paper and pencils/felt tip pens
Dark chocolate

Centring music

Music chosen by the group, to help them focus on the theme, was played.

The candle was lit.

Introduction

Although being a mother is central for many women for part of their lives, it is only rarely celebrated in women's liturgy groups or in collections of experiential worship. This may partly be because there has been a reaction against having one's identity defined in terms of being a mother, a wife, a daughter and so on. Another reason might be because there are many women in our midst who have not given physical birth.

This last, however, overlooks the aspect of people 'giving birth' to all sorts of creativity, not only in the arts but in their relationships and work, including the nurturing help for other adults which women are so often involved in.

It is easy to be unrealistic about being a mother. As well as the joys and enrichment many mothers experience, it is also a process that brings much exhaustion and anxiety. Tonight we bring all our own varied experiences – we have all had mothers, and we are all called on to nurture others and to connect with them, for in essence our lives are a reflection of the motherly aspects of the divine.

Song

'Dear Mother God'
(Janet Wootton in *Reflecting Praise*)

Discussion (in pairs or threes)

What are your experiences of being mothered/mothering or nurturing? Are there painful aspects you want to leave behind you? What were/are the good aspects?

Rejection of the Painful

Participants, if they so wished, threw a small stone into a small bin, praying out loud or silently about what this represented. This was accompanied by silent reflection asking for help in forgiving others for these hurts, or for forgiveness of the hurts they had themselves given.

Rejoicing in the Good Aspects

Flowerheads were placed in a bowl of water, each person offering a prayer of thanksgiving, aloud or silently.

Prayer

God the Motherer,
The all-nurturing
Source of all loving relationship.
Empowering,
Growth evoking,
Supportive yet releasing;

Creation sharing,
Shelter in the dark,
Impelling onwards the light,
Strengthener and comforter;

Mirrored in the love that enriches,
In the times of shadow,
Sustain us when the journey becomes hard.
(Ianthe Pratt)

Collect

'God our mother, you hold our life within you'
(Janet Morley in *All Desires Known*)

Discussion (in pairs or threes)

What does the mothering image of the divine mean to you?

Haikus on some aspect of motherhood/nurturance/female aspects of the divine were written. (These poems take the form of 5–7–5 syllables, though the form should not be imposed so severely as to restrict creativity. For an example of a haiku see 'Images of God', page 110.)

These were then placed in the centre, after being read out if participants wished.

Sharing of Food

Leader   We share today dark chocolate, which is sweet, sustaining, and medically beneficial.

Each person in turn broke off some, offered it to the next one, saying, 'May this food sustain you on your journey of life.'

Song (tune: Quem Pastores)

'Mary's Journey'
(*In Praise of All Encircling Love*, Vol. 1, see also page 153 above).

The liturgy ended with a circle dance.

28

Women and Justice

No apology is needed for including yet another liturgy, this time particularly based on scripture, on the subject of justice and women.

Elements

Candles

Introduction

Reading

Leviticus 25:1–19 (Restitution and Jubilee)

A candle was lit for the Sabbath.

Discussion

What could marking the Sabbath mean for women?

Litany (said antiphonally)

A   Blow the trumpet and proclaim the Sabbath.
B   Blow the trumpet and proclaim a feast.
A   The Sabbath has come, our time of rest,
B   Our time of healing and wholeness and rest.
A   On the Sabbath all of creation rests,
B   All creatures are equal because all will rest.
A   Praise our God, who calls us to make our lives simple.
B   To live simply and sanely as children of God.

A candle was lit for the forgiveness of debts.

Discussion

What could the forgiveness of debts mean for women?

Song

'O Healing River' (first verse)
(Fran Minkoff, Appleseed Music Inc.)

A candle was lit for letting the land lie fallow.

Discussion

What could 'lying fallow' mean for women?

Song

'O Healing River' (second verse)

A candle was lit for freedom and liberty.

Discussion

What could freedom mean for women?

Song

'O Healing River' (third verse)

A candle was lit for celebration (in this instance the celebration was of Jubilee, but a group might have other reasons to celebrate).

Litany (said antiphonally)

A   Let everyone say 'Yes' to the future,
      Let everyone say 'Yes' to the future,

B   A future of healing, of hope, of new life,
New life for all of creation.

A   Say 'Yes' to justice and reconciliation,
Justice for all in the presence of God.

B   Let everyone say 'Yes' to the spirit of Wisdom,
For we are made in the image of Wisdom,

A   We spread a banquet and call to our children,
We bind up wounds and soothe away fear,

B   And we live in the hope of resurrection,
Today, tomorrow, and forever.

All **Amen.**

Song (tune: Londonderry Air)

'We shall go out with hope of resurrection'
(June Boyce-Tillman)

Resources

Use of Resources

While there should be room for spontaneity in such things as free-form prayer and interactive reflections between the participants, it is often helpful to include material from other sources. There is, however, a tendency for people leading the liturgy to leave things to the last minute, and this can lead to overdependence on the ideas of others. Preferably each liturgy should contain at least some new material worked out specially for the occasion.

Biblical Material

The Inclusive New Testament, Priests for Equality (USA).
A fresh dynamic translation which goes further into inclusivity than other versions.
There is also an *Inclusive Language Lectionary*, 3 volumes for years A–C, National Council of Churches of Christ (USA).

A number of new editions of Bibles such as the *New Jerusalem Bible*, the *New Revised Standard Version* and the *Revised English Bible* have made minor changes to make them more inclusive; this generally only extends to the community and not to the divine.

Much used are Jim Cotter's version of the Psalms, *Through Desert Places* (Psalms 1–50), some free-form and *By Stony Paths* (Psalms 51–100), and *Towards the City* (Psalms 101–150). Many people favour the American Carmelite *New Companion to the Breviary*, which is a short inclusive edition. There is also the *New Companion to the Breviary with Seasonal Supplement*, and accompanying *Scripture Readings*, 2 volumes (1989) covering the liturgical year. Many of the collections of prayer below are based on the Scriptures.

Resources

Collections of Prayers and Liturgies

Blessings of Food and Drink in Creative Worship, London: Christian Women's Resource Centre, 1988.
Background to the *agape*, different forms and responses.

Celebrating One World: Worship Resource on Social Justice, London: Collins, Fount, 1988.
The CAFOD collection of prayers, reflections, songs and poems from around the world.

In Spirit and In Truth, World Council of Churches, Canberra Assembly book, Geneva: WCC, 1991.
Prayers, hymns and responses which use inclusive language.

Journey to the Millennium and Beyond, National Board of Catholic Women, Wakering, Essex: McCrimmon, Great 1998.
An ecumenical collection of reflections, prayers and poems contributed by Christian women. There is much insight here which should be useful for personal and group use, but some of the language is traditional.

The Pattern of Our Days: Liturgies and Resources for Worship, Glasgow: Wild Goose Publications, 1996.
An anthology reflecting the life and witness of the Iona Community. See also their journal *Coracle* which often contains poems and liturgies. This can be obtained from the Iona Community, 840 Govan Rd, Glasgow, G51 3UU.

Prayers and Psalms, London: St Joan's International Alliance (GB section), 1998.
These have been collected from their meetings and liturgies.

Christine Allen and Barbara D'Arcy (eds), *The Trampled Vineyard*, London: CHAS/Unleash, 1992.
An anthology of worship resources on housing, homelessness and social justice.

Simon Bryden-Brook (ed.), *Take, Bless, Break, Share*, Norwich: Canterbury Press, 1998.
A collection of *agapes*, table blessings and liturgies, mainly in inclusive language. These vary in their formality.

Jim Cotter, *Prayer at Night's Approaching*, Sheffield: Cairns, 1997.
An expanded small format edition of *Prayer at Night* (which is still available). This is an excellent selection using inclusive language. Much of it is newly written.
Also by Jim Cotter: *Prayer in the Morning and Healing – More or Less*, Sheffield: Cairns, 1987.

Iben Gjerding and Katherine Kinnamon (eds), *No Longer Strangers: A Resource for Women and Worship*, Geneva: WCC, 1984.
One of the earliest collections, now out of print but worth searching for.

Janet Morley, *All Desires Known*, second extended edition, London: SPCK, 1988.
Alternative collects, litanies, canticles, eucharistic prayers. A valuable collection from the pen of one of the foremost writers of prayers today, using the experience of women.

Janet Morley (ed.), *Bread of Tomorrow*, London: SPCK/Christian Aid, 1993.
Subtitled 'Praying with the world's poor', this is an enriching collection of prayers, poems and meditations.

Janet Morley, Hannah Ward and Jennifer Wild (eds), *Celebrating Women*, London: SPCK, 1995.
An expanded edition of this pioneering collection of women's prayer and liturgy.

Rosemary Radford Ruether, *Woman Church*, San Francisco: Harper & Row, 1985.
This includes a variety of rites and liturgies as well as theoretical discussion.

Elizabeth Roberts and Elias Amidon, *Earth Prayers*, San Francisco: Harper, 1991.
A collection with a global outlook.

St Hilda's Community, *The New Women Included*, London: SPCK, 1996.
The updated edition of the worship material from the community, with new introductory chapters. This is an invaluable aid for worship groups.

Janet R. Walton, *Feminist Liturgy: A Matter of Justice*, Collegeville: Liturgical Press, 2000.
An insightful introduction to the theory and process of feminist liturgy with a number of liturgies for the stages and events of women's lives.

Hannah Ward and Jennifer Wild (eds), *Human Rites: Worship resources for an age of change*, London: Mowbray, 1995.
An ecumenical collection of prayers, liturgies and rituals springing from the creativity of individuals and groups.

Sources of Readings

Tissa Balisuriya, *Mary and Human Liberation*, London: Cassell, 1997.
Useful for rethinking on Mary, Mother of God.

Leonardo and Clodovis Boff, *Introducing Liberation Theology*, London: Burns & Oates, 1987.

Barbara Bowe and others (eds), *Silent Voices Sacred Lives*, New York: Paulist Press, 1986.
Women's readings for the liturgical year.

Helder Camara, *The Desert is Fertile*, London: Sheed & Ward, 1974.
Out of print but worth searching for, particularly for justice themes.

Sydney Carter, *In the Present Tense*, Vol. 1, London: Stainer & Bell, 1996.
This contains among other items to be read or sung, 'Judas and Mary' and 'The Bird of Heaven'. A CD is also available: *Sydney Carter's Lord of the Dance: 26 Poems and Songs*, Stainer & Bell, London 1996 (CD0087).

Joan Chittister, *The Heart of Flesh: A Feminist Spirituality for Women and Men*, Grand Rapids: Eerdmans, 1998.
Much useful material on the breakdown of society and the means for renewal.

Church of England Board for Social Responsibility, *Cybernauts Awake!*, London: Church House Publishing, 1999.

Kathy Galloway, *Love Burning Deep*, London: SPCK, 1993.

Kathy Galloway (ed.), *Pushing the Boat Out*, Glasgow: Wild Goose Publications, 1995.
A collection of poetry by twelve women and four men who are concerned with the work of the Iona Community.

Edwina Gately, *Psalms of a Laywoman*, Franklin, Wisconsin: Sheed & Ward, 1999.
A new collection of these insightful reflections.

Janice Grana (ed.), *Images: Women in transition*, Winona, Massachusetts: St Mary's Press, 1991.
Poetry, prose and pictures under headings of identity, freedom, the needs of others, the rhythms of life, the presence of God, pain and sorrow, work and service, the future.

Amanda Hopkinson (ed.), *Lovers and Comrades: Wilderness Resistance Poetry*, London: Women's Press, 1989.
Translated by Amanda Hopkinson and members of the El Salvador Solidarity Campaign Cultural Committee.

Sara Juengst, *Like a Garden*, Philadelphia: Westminster Press, 1996.
A biblical spirituality of growth.

Hans Küng and Jürgen Moltmann (eds), *Mary in the Churches*, Concilium 168, Edinburgh: T. & T. Clark, 1983.

Elisabeth Moltmann-Wendel, *The Women around Jesus*, London: SCM Press, 1982.
Now out of print but worth borrowing.

Rosemary Radford Ruether, *Sexism and God-Talk: Towards a Feminist Theology*, London: SCM Press, 1983.
A standard book on the subject that has much that is quotable.

Ian Reid, *Meditations from the Iona Community*, Glasgow: Wild Goose Publications, 1998.
A useful collection, mainly using inclusive language, about both the community and the divine.

Douglas Rhymes, *Prayer in the Secular City*, Philadelphia: Westminster Press, 1967.

Adrienne Rich, *The Fact of a Doorframe*, New York: Norton, 1981.

Sandra Schneiders, *Women and the Word*, New York: Paulist Press, 1986.
Insights on the way we speak of the divine.

Nicola Slee, *The Easter Garden*, London: Collins, Fount, 1990.
Poems and prose.

W. H. Vanstone, *The Stature of Waiting*, London: Darton, Longman & Todd, 1982.

Hannah Ward and Jennifer Wild (eds), *Conversations*, London: SPCK, 1997.
Meeting our forebears in faith.

Simone Weil, *Waiting on God*, London: Collins, Fontana, 1973.

Brian Woodcock and Jan Sutch Pickard, *Advent Readings from Iona*, Glasgow: Wild Goose Publications, 2000.

Sheet Liturgies

A list of sheet liturgies is available from the Christian Women's Resource Centre (see address on p. 188).

Music

Hymns Old and New, melody edition, Great Wakering: McCrimmon, 1984 (later editions available).
A source, among other hymn books, of some of the songs used in the liturgies in this book.

Iona Abbey is a source of much relevant music (Wild Goose Publications). The following are particularly recommended:

Wild Goose Songs, Vols 1, 2 and 3; *Many and Great* and *Sent by the Lord* (Songs from around the world, Vols I and II); *Psalms of Patience, Protest and Praise*; *Innkeepers and Light Sleepers* (for Christmas); and *The Last Journey: Reflections for a Time of Grieving*, John Bell. Most of these also have tapes and CDs. A list of tapes is available from the Association for Inclusive Language at the same address as Lumen Books (see below).

Songs and Hymns of Fellowship, Eastbourne: Kingsway Publishers, 1985.

Sounds of Living Waters, B. Pulkingham and J. Harper, London: Hodder and Stoughton, 1977.

Twenty-four Psalms and a Canticle, The Grail/Gelinau Gregorian Institute of America, Chicago, 1983, available in Britain from Decani Music, 30 North Terrace, Mildenhall IP28 7AB, 1955.
The Grail psalms are a good quarry, but earlier versions do not have inclusive language.

Resources

June Boyce-Tillman, *In Praise of All Encircling Love*, Vols 1 and 2, London: Association for Inclusive Language/Hildegard Press, 1992 and 1995.
A wide variety of inclusive language songs for different occasions. Some have new words to familiar tunes, many have new music and words. A taped meditation on Hildegard of Bingen and CDs are also available.

June Boyce-Tillman and Janet Wootton (eds), *Reflecting Praise*, London: Stainer & Bell/WIT, 1993.
A wide ranging collection.

Kevin Mayhew (ed.), *The Complete Celebration Hymnbook*, Great Wakering: McCrimmon, 1989.

Gabriele Uhlein, *Meditations with Hildegard of Bingen*, Santa Fe, Mexico: Bear, 1983.
A 'greening' selection useful for creative worship.

Paul Winter, *Missa Gaia: Earth Mass*, Litchfield, USA: Living Music Records, 1987.
A useful cassette for liturgies on a theme of nature.

Brian Wren, *Praising a Mystery* and *Bring Many Names*, Carol Stream, Illinois: Hope Publishing, 1986 and 1989.
These develop a rich imagery of God and give the music of the songs to be found in his *What Language Shall I Borrow?*

Further Explorations

Network, the journal of the Catholic Women's Network is published quarterly and can be obtained from: Ann Farr, 49 Stanley Road, Earlsdon, Coventry, CV5 6FG.

Among the books and materials helpful in the discussion of creative worship and inclusive language are:

Inclusive Language and Imagery about God, Peterborough: Methodist Publishing House, 1996.

Gillian Limb, Veronica Seddon and Mairin Valdez, *Death and Renewal of Creation: A Women's Easter Experience*, London: Catholic Women's Network, 2001.

Ianthe Pratt, *Inclusive Language – Faith Community – God Talk – Creative Worship*, distance learning module produced by the British and Irish School of Feminist Theology.

Marjorie Proctor Smith, *Praying with Our Eyes Open: Engendering Feminist Liturgical Prayer*, Nashville: Abingdon Press, 1995.

Gail Ramshaw, *God Beyond Gender: Feminist Christian God-Language*, Minneapolis: Fortress Press, 1995.

Letty Russell, *The Liberating Word*, Philadelphia: Westminster Press, 1976.

Brian Wren, *What Language Shall I Borrow?*, London: SCM Press, 1989.

The following books take further the study of the development of feminist theology:

Trafficking in Women in Europe: Papers from an International Consultation, Driebergen, Netherlands: Conference of European Churches, 1999.

Carol Christ, *Diving Deep and Surfacing: Women Writers on Spiritual Quest*, Boston: Beacon Press, 1980.

Chung Hyun Kyung, *Struggle to be the Sun Again: Introducing Asian Women's Theology*, London: SCM Press, 1990.

Virginia M. M. Fabella and Sergio Torres (eds), *Irruption of the Third World: Challenge to Theology*, Maryknoll, New York: Orbis Books, 1983.

Elizabeth Schüssler Fiorenza, *Bread not Stone: The Challenge of Feminist Biblical Interpretation*, Boston: Beacon Press, 1984.

Ann Gary and Marilyn Pearsall, *Women, Knowledge and Reality, Explorations in Feminist Philosophy*, Boston: Unwin Hyman, 1989.

Aruna Gnanadason, *Living Letter: A Report of Visits to the Churches during the Ecumenical Decade for Churches in Solidarity with Women*, Geneva: WCC Publications, 1997.

Aruna Gnanadason, *No Longer a Secret: The church and violence against women*, Geneva: WCC Publications, revised edition, 1997.

Mary Grey, *Redeeming the Dream: Feminism, Redemption and the Christian Tradition*, London: SPCK, 1989.

Lisa Isherwood and Dorothea McEwan (eds), *An A–Z of Feminist Theology*, Sheffield: Sheffield Academic Press, 1996.

Lisa Isherwood and Elizabeth Stuart, *Body Theology*, Sheffield: Sheffield Academic Press, 1998.

Rosemary Radford Ruether, *Religion and Sexism: Images of Women in the Jewish and Christian Traditions*, New York: Simon & Schuster, 1974.
Adrienne Rich, *What is Found There: Notebooks on Poetry and Politics*, New York: Norton, 1993.

Elizabeth Stuart, *Religion is a Queer Thing*, London: Cassell, 1998.

Emilie M. Townes (ed.), *A Troubling In My Soul: Womanist Perspectives On Evil and Suffering*, Maryknoll, New York: Orbis Books, 1993.

The resources suggested here are only a small selection from the full annotated booklist which can be obtained from the Christian Women's Resource Centre, Lumen Religious Books Trust, 36 Court Lane, London SE21 7DR (telephone/fax 020 8693 1438; e-mail *Lumen@globalnet.co.uk*).

The Liturgy section of the Reference Library at the Centre (CWRC) is held jointly with the Association for Inclusive Language which can give advice and information to inquirers. The Association's Bulletin also often includes experiential liturgies. If you have difficulty in obtaining books and materials locally, most of the items referred to are available for sale at the Centre, personally or by post. It is necessary to make an appointment before visiting.

Acknowledgments

The groups responsible for producing the liturgies reproduced here were:

Catholic Women's Network (CWN) – Liturgies: 7 Passover, 8 Easter (with St Joan's), 12 Seeing, 13 Fire, Air, Water and Earth, 15 Justice, 17 Wilderness, 18 Anger and Peace (with WELG), 21 Journeying, 24 Honouring Our Foremothers, 25 'Croning', 26 Menstruation and Menopause and 27 Mothering and Nurturing.

Catholic Women's Ordination – Liturgies: 3 Epiphany, 4 Annunciation: Women's World Day of Prayer, 5 Annunciation and 6 Maundy Thursday

St Joan's International Alliance – Liturgies: 8 Easter (with CWN), 14 Balance, 16 Leadership, 20 Facing Change, 22 Reclaiming Mary and 23 Reclaiming Mary Magdalene.

Wimbledon Experimental Liturgy Group (WELG) – Liturgies: 1 Advent: Advent Wreath, 9 Pentecost, 11 Images of God and 18 Anger and Peace (with Catholic Women's Network).

Wherwell Liturgy Group – Liturgies: 2 New Year and Epiphany, 10 Harvest, 19 A Shared Meal and 28 Women and Justice.

We are grateful to the following for permission to reproduce material:

Churches Together in Britain and Ireland for the poem 'Making Liturgy' by Ruth Burgess from Ruth Harvey (ed.), *Wrestling and Resting* (p. viii); Wild Goose Publications for the poem 'Credo' by Ruth Burgess from Kathy Galloway (ed.), *Pushing the Boat Out* (p. 134); Diann Neu, Co-Director of WATER, the Women's Alliance for Theology, Ethics and Ritual, 8035 13th Street, Silver Spring, MD 20910, USA for her prayer, 'This is the season of hope!' from *Blessed Be the New Year: A Ritual of Hope*, a liturgy used in December 1992 (p. 62); Sr Kira Sohldoost for her prayer 'Come, be with us' (p. 141); Sara Ingles for her prayer 'Be thou my guardian' (pp. 142–3).